T0266200

'The challenges of translating elaborate poems from Persian to modern English are legion, especially when has bravely set out to imitate the intense and comple beauty of the originals in a new language. But Mario Petrucci takes on the task with gusto here, and is to be applauded.'

HENRY SHUKMAN, poet, novelist, Zen teacher,
author of *Archangel* (Cape Poetry, 2013)

'Petrucci's adaptations are a delight to read. They are fresh, candid, subtly humorous, and elegant. They have that audacious and multi-layered richness one finds in the originals. Above all, they are uncompromising. Petrucci has clearly worked to form an under-standing of Hafez's vision, artistry and devotional ambience, and he goes to the necessary length to let all that shine through.'

FATEMEH KESHAVARZ, Director and Chair,
Roshan Institute for Persian Studies, University of Maryland

'Mario Petrucci's new versions of Hafez are nuanced and thoughtful, embracing both the depth and the beauty of the original. These renditions also allow us to take stock while we read, the words never slipping lyrically through our intellectual grasp.'

SASHA DUGDALE, Editor, *Modern Poetry in Translation*

'Petrucci bases his engagement with Hafez on a special awareness, one that goes deeper than mere understanding of content to a com-prehension of the "Union" that Hafez reveals. Everywhere, his deli-cate but probing selection of word and phrase uplifts and inspires.'

MICHAEL *HAKUZAN* WENNINGER, Zen monk

'An incredible ride. A Ferris wheel for the heart and mind.'

ADAM SIMMONDS, Kabbalistic teacher

Hafez is among the most celebrated of Persian mystic poets, thriving alongside such towering figures as Rumi and Saadi. Ubiquitous in Iran, he has also carried significant influence in the West. These eighty-one poems, selected from his most potent ghazals, reflect his remarkable spiritual trajectory: two epic vigils, separated by forty years, which led to God-realisation. Interpreted variously as ardent mystic and lover, Hafez fuses earthly and divine love with an intense constancy as memorably productive as Dante's courtly adoration for Beatrice. *Beloved* sets out to reanimate that exquisite convergence between the human and the cosmic.

No translator can convey, in full, the seemingly limitless devotion and alert endurance of Hafez or capture, completely, the master poet's immaculate musicality, his rich complexity. Nevertheless, with ingenuity and vigour, Petrucci leaps the obstacles of time and culture to provide, in English, an authentic and accessible modern rendering of the Persian. Sensitive to the moral clarity and sensual abundance of his source, he mobilises a radiant lyricism in service to the ageless linguistic beauty of the originals. *Beloved* joins the irresistible force that is Hafez, whose healing wisdom, honesty and exuberance continue to percolate into the intimate consciousness of so many.

Beloved

81 POEMS FROM
HAFEZ

translated by
MARIO PETRUCCI

with forewords by
FATEMEH KESHAVARZ
& MICHAEL WENNINGER

BLOODAXE BOOKS

Copyright © Mario Petrucci 2018

ISBN: 978 1 78037 430 7

First published 2018 by
Bloodaxe Books Ltd,
Eastburn,
South Park,
Hexham,
Northumberland NE46 1BS.

www.bloodaxebooks.com
For further information about Bloodaxe titles
please visit our website or write to
the above address for a catalogue.

Cover design: Neil Astley & Pamela Robertson-Pearce.

Digital reprint of the 2018 Bloodaxe Books edition.

ACKNOWLEDGEMENTS

I'm deeply indebted to Lieut.-Col. H. Wilberforce Clarke, who embraced the gargantuan task of creating something akin to an English "urtext" for the Divan of Hafez 'amidst the pressure and the stress of professional duties most exacting; and under special circumstances of harass and worry that it is not permissible to describe' [Clarke (1891), Preface xvi].

I thank Manjusri for her support and love, and for her many comments on this work – her innate insight and clarity on the essential qualities of Hafez's poetry proved invaluable. I'm grateful to Peter Brennan for his wise confirmatory eye, and to Mahtab Clark for answering certain queries concerning the *coda* poem.

Thanks are also due to the editors of the following publications and websites where some of these poems first appeared: *Anima*, *Columbia Journal* (columbiajournal.org), *International Times* (http://international times.it), *Irish Pages* (Belfast), *Meniscus* (www.meniscus.org.au), *Modern Poetry in Translation*, *Plumwood Mountain* (Australia; https://plumwoodmountain.com), *Poems for a Liminal Age* (SPM Publications, 2015), *Presence* (USA), *Prosopisia* (India), *Resurgence & Ecologist*, *Stand*, *The Ghazal Page* (ghazalpage.org), *The Moth* (Ireland).

The Emerson quotation (on Hafez) that frames my Preface uses the wording given in: *The Complete Works of Ralph Waldo Emerson, with a Biographical Introduction and Notes by Edward Waldo Emerson and a General Index [Volume VIII: Letters and Social Aims]*; Houghton, Mifflin and Company (Boston and New York, 1904).

Front cover image: folio from a Divan by Hafez (16th century).
Back cover image: *Vigil* (2014); artwork by Mario Petrucci (pencil & crayon on paper).

CONTENTS

for the One

FOREWORD

by FATEMEH KESHAVARZ

Director and Chair, Roshan Institute for Persian Studies,
University of Maryland

When I was eight or nine, my grandmother gave me a pack of cards with poorly imitated Persian miniature paintings on one side, and a ghazal by Hafez printed on the other. I tried to read the poems between attempts to build houses with the cards. There was much that was hard to tackle in the poetry, but even the large and unfamiliar words felt delicious to the tongue. And they had comforting rhythm. That is how I memorised many ghazals without much conscious effort. Later in my childhood, I strolled in the garden of Hafez's mausoleum, ten minutes away from our house in Shiraz, and studied for high school tests, taking utterly for granted the fact that hundreds of people visited daily to pay their respects. Surely all great poets had that?

Those visiting his mausoleum whispered words of prayer under their breath and carried his book of poetry almost with the same reverence with which one would carry holy books. And yet, where his poems were recited and discussed, there would always be heated debates often leading to one question, the one persisting to this day: 'Did Hafez speak of *real* wine – or was his wine evocative of spiritual intoxication?' It took me a long while to do away with the "either/or" inherent in the question and realise that the great appeal Hafez has is in his uncanny ability to connect heaven and earth as though they should never have been imagined as separate. That is, one is not supposed to be sure if the ruby red wine that he drank came out of jars or was fermented in paradise. This uncertainty is at the heart of Hafez's magic: his poetry is unsurpassed in its ability to embrace the ambiguity, to live with the unknowing and to let it be productive in us in any way it chooses.

The topic of translating Hafez's colourful and daring poems into another language did not come up for me until graduate school. There were a number of English translations with varying degrees of success. Did the calibre of the art make it untranslatable? Many scholars of Persian heritage would say it did. How far could one go to express, in English, the poetic rigour and complexity without being disloyal to the original (to evoke a classic anxiety of translators)? Hafez himself had been bold in his poetic ventures; I craved for an equivalent courage in the translations that I read. Not surprisingly, few would go far enough. Years passed. Then, a few months ago, I received a manu-script for *Beloved: 81 poems from Hafez*, the poetic renderings of a selection of the ghazals, by Mario Petrucci.

Regarding the method he had used, Petrucci wrote: 'There were so many variants of the poems in English, and the order in which they come, that I eventually settled on the old 1891 literal English versions by Wilberforce Clarke. That's the text I mainly worked from. I lis-tened to the Persian by several means to gauge its sonic spirit, and I looked at original Persian texts with their various English translations to get a grip on shape, content and tone...'

I was not quite sure how to feel about basing the work on prose translations carried out over a century ago. But any genuine poetic grappling with Hafez is worth a genuine reading, and I decided to ap-proach these renderings in a spirit of unknowing, allowing the poems to enter and reveal themselves the way they chose to. By the third or fourth ghazal, the unknowing had transformed into a pleasing surprise; by the tenth poem, I was energised; beyond that, I was thrilled enough to not count any more. So, I played a fun game. I decided to gauge the loyalty of the renderings by reading each poem without the original Persian in front of me, to see how far I needed to go before I recog-nised each poem. Often it was the first or the second verse. Only in one case did I fail to identify the ghazal. In this collection, the echo of Hafez's voice was unmistakable.

Petrucci's adaptations are a delight to read. They are fresh, candid, subtly humorous, and elegant. They have that audacious and multi-layered richness one finds in the originals. Above all, they are uncompromising. Petrucci has clearly worked to form an understanding of Hafez's vision, artistry and devotional ambience, and he goes to the necessary length to let all that shine through.

FOREWORD

by MICHAEL *HAKUZAN* WENNINGER

Zen monk

After carefully laying out the rice paper, the master calligrapher takes the inkstone and slowly grinds the inkstick with water. When the proper mixture is achieved, he dips his brush. With the brush hovering over the paper in perfect meditative response, the master patiently waits for that unspoken moment when brush, ink, paper and artist merge into One. This "unpredictability", when it finally arrives, releases the brush. In that movement of not-doing, master and brush – guided by some unseen *Something* – flow, to create an impeccable expression of *It*. Only years of practice and untiring devotion can bring the mastery that transcends technique. Only when an artist becomes the Artless Artist can the Nameless be suggested or implied.

In his own journey to becoming the Artless Artist, Hafez was as meticulous – and as alive – as that master calligrapher. His words are delightful brushstrokes, a flowing of spiritual subtleties that unbinds us from ourselves. By removing the veil of superficiality, his poetry escapes time and space, opening a gateway beyond mind and body to some deeply unified place in our Beingness. In *Beloved*, we glimpse the cloth, 'damp with Love', that clears the dust from our mirror, lifting the illusion of separation from Grace.

What makes this realisation of ultimate inseparability more possible, for a Western reader, is Mario Petrucci's rendering. Petrucci bases his engagement with Hafez on a special awareness, one that goes deeper than mere understanding of content to a comprehension of the "Union" that Hafez reveals. Everywhere, his delicate but probing selection of word and phrase uplifts and inspires, leaving the indelible imprint of a *Something* that can't be described intellectually, only experienced. This imprinting of that hidden *Something* is the preciousness of Petrucci's gift.

TRANSLATOR'S PREFACE

'Nothing stops him; he makes the dare-God and dare-devil experiment…
he fears nothing, he sees too far, and sees throughout.'

RALPH WALDO EMERSON

'There is as much sense in Hafiz as in Horace,
and as much knowledge of the world.'

SHERLOCK HOLMES

The verifiable biography for Hafez is sparse, but easily found, so needs no repeating here. The aggregation of stories and sayings surrounding this remarkable 14th century Persian poet, however, is markedly bulkier and, I suspect, steeply inclined towards what tradition demands of rhetoric rather than banal fact. One facet of the poet's "biography" (whether true or supposed) that has communicated itself powerfully into this collection is the symmetry of his spiritual trajectory as told through the following 'mythical anecdote' (Gertrude Bell's phrase). Hafez entered upon two, hugely demanding vigils separated by forty years. The first was spurred by his love for a young woman; it lasted forty nights and led to his becoming a disciple of Attar (not to be confused with Attar the famous poet). The second vigil, more exacting still, entailed forty days and nights sitting within a circle he had himself drawn on the ground. It arose from his desperation at his (perceived) long separation from God, and it resulted in his God-realisation. This story orchestrates the organisation of *Beloved*. The first forty poems, gathered together in the section entitled *The Thirst*, reflect an intense yearning to merge with the Beloved, a searching and sometimes distraught voice that seeks "the wine" through adversity and apparent estrangement. The second half of the book, *The Slaking*, also comprising forty poems, suggests a more enraptured spirit in cosmic union, partaking gratefully of Love and Selfhood, whether caught up in praise or offering sage meditations on the soul's condition. Naturally, this sweeping division of emphasis is neither unambiguous nor strictly adhered to within the poems themselves: *Slaking* and *Thirst*, here, are convenient labels that encompass a variety of vintages and hues relating to the highs and lows of the spiritual journey. To close the book, providing the capstone for the above structure, there is a single poem: my version of the ghazal that forms part of the inscription on Hafez's tomb in Shiraz.

Commentators have pointed to the fraught question of whether Hafez meant his poetry to be understood in largely literal or mystical terms. This problem is clouded by the observation that all Persian poets of his era were working in a literary tradition where the vocabulary and metaphors of mysticism and lyricism had mostly coalesced. I'm of the opinion that Hafez was constitutionally devotional; I was thus inclined – as was Clarke, my prime source (see below) – to admit a Sufistic perspective when translating him. That said, it would also seem that Hafez was very much involved in the world, and that he revelled in the aforementioned convergence between the language of heaven and of earth, exploiting the linguistic ambiguities to the full. I've been careful, then, to ensure that the poetry's more corporeal and temporal resonances haven't been unduly excluded or quelled. I adopted the above strategy fairly evenly throughout this book, even though one imagines that the poems of the younger, love-struck man might well have been more strongly secular. My main reason for doing this arises from the snag that Hafez's Divan isn't ordered chronologically, making it troublesome to pin down the poems' positions relative to his biography or to ascertain how, exactly, the weighting between his worldly and heavenly intentions may have shifted as he matured in years and insight.

A more mundane issue that steered this volume was my reluctance to include poems that contained conspicuous references (to people, places, stories, etc.) that would be unfamiliar to most modern readers, and that would consequently need explicit, possibly even extensive, footnoting. On those occasions, though, where the presence of one or more obscure names in an original couldn't dissuade me from taking that particular poem on, I reconstructed and reconnected each reference towards an abundant simplicity that seemed, to me, easier to assimilate and fitting to the context. Failing that, I did what I could to make sure that the reference was used in such a way that its gist was relatively obvious. These decisions were helpful in sidestepping the considerable industry of Hafez commentary that, over time, has most usefully burgeoned and upon which some readers thrive. I don't underestimate the value of supporting material in generating a fuller appreciation of the subtlety of Hafez's wit and sensibility; but the scholarly or specialist detail that haloes the poetry (with its concomitant discussions and disputes) isn't something I wanted to make central here, in what I envisaged as a relatively "clean", stand-alone selection of Hafez's surviving work.

Many texts were consulted in the writing of these poems, but my principal sources were:

> *The Divan-i-Hafiz*, translated by Lieut.-Col. H. Wilberforce **Clarke** (Calcutta, 1891);
> *Divan of Hafiz*, translated by Paul **Smith** (New Humanity Books / CreateSpace, 2012);
> *The Hafez Poems of Gertrude Bell*, by G. Lowthian **Bell** (Iranbooks / Ibex, 1995).

Of these, it was Clarke's text that I followed most closely. His conversion of Hafez's poetry into English prose (in two volumes, with 'critical and explanatory remarks') was indispensable to me. Where different translations were found to be in discrepancy, I broadly stuck – rightly or wrongly, and often for consistency's sake – with Clarke. This would, I knew, compromise any impeccable academic precision I might tentatively have wished for; but it was self-evident, anyway, that a certain amount of phrase-making and poetic improvisation was inevitable, owing to the literal prose of Clarke's translation that comes festooned with notes and interpretative alternatives. Moreover, although I trusted that the bulk of my work would be based (through Clarke) on originals that came from Hafez's own hand, it was clear from the body of research that accompanies Hafez's oeuvre that the authentication and most valid deciphering of words, couplets and even entire poems can be problematic, to say the least, and is quite rightly a subject for continuing debate. There's little doubt that Clarke's text itself isn't flawless in this regard. I'm equally convinced that a preoccupation with the problem was inessential in a project of this kind. Any sustained attempt on my part at absolute academic rigour would have also courted (putting it metaphorically) the willing placement of two mirrors face to face with my sanity and livelihood caught between.

What's more, the enterprise of converting Hafez into modern, vibrant English necessarily entails incidental inaccuracies and anachronisms of reference and diction: these unavoidably seep in, either directly or by implication. I minimised all such distortions wherever I could, but stopped short of becoming too obsessive over such issues as, say, the detailed historical veracity of the poems' references. *Beloved* isn't concerned, after all, with a forensic fidelity to Hafez's time; its aesthetic, rather, has been to deploy all the appropriate poetic resources of our own age so as to capture, as far as possible, the spirit of an ancient poetic master. This translation therefore emerged as something more personal and energetic than one that's "faithful to the letter". In fact, I preferred to allow myself some latitude, devising (where I was moved to do so) a number of phrasings, allusions and images that aren't wholly present in the originals. These were designed, in part, to compensate for the extraordinary vitality and thoughtful spontaneity of the Persian being seldom transferred intact into English. They were also a response to English having, arguably, a more image-centred poetic tradition than ancient Persia. Other lines and figures of speech were altered towards greater accord with the considerations and imagery around them, a bias in keeping with the feel of this particular book.

I resolved, too, to vary specific symbolic combinations – such as the candle and the moth, and the nightingale and the rose – away from their standard forms of presentation in the originals, thereby softening the edges of (what might seem to an English ear) some of the more insistent furrows of Persian convention. On top of this, I sprinkled Hafez (albeit sparingly) with some of my own gentle links to the classical Western canon. One couplet, for instance, refers to E. V. Rieu's version of the Odyssey through the phrase 'glossy burden'; another couplet draws on Dante, with '…the ninth heaven, quickened, burnt/ in the ways of God' arising from *Paradiso* XXIII, 112-14; in a third couplet, I summon a stag to join the cypress rooted in my Hafez source text, thus hinting at the story of Cyparissus, the youth transformed into the tree because of his profound grief at having inadvertently killed a cherished stag. There were many other means by which individual poems were reconfigured to take advantage of the leniencies of a modern translation, as with the *coda* piece, where the unflagging refrain in Clarke/ Hafez ('I rise'/ 'I may rise') was modulated to a series of more varied, upward gestures. At every turn, I tried to be creative and flexible when adapting the poetry for wider readership, as well as in staying alert to how best to connect us to Hafez's world (as depicted via Clarke's version). In *Beloved 22*, for example, 'sacred house' and 'black-stone' bring the Ka'ba (in Mecca) into the poem, as required, but do so less fixedly by not naming it, while 'Recite yourself' profits from the etymological coupling that exists between the words *recitation* and *Qur'an*. *Beloved 80*, meanwhile, with the phrase 'see the world both whole and passing', introduces (in an aptly slant manner) the powers associated with the cup of Jamshid, 'the revealer of the mystery of time and of Earth' (Clarke, p.31). And so on.

All of these adaptations, extensions and insertions are alive, I hope, to Hafez's thrust and tone, but they nevertheless remain (to various extents) my own invention. It's also true that, here and there, small parts of the originals weren't taken forward into my versions at all; but, I stress, these "exclusions" were never grievous. They were usually allowed in order to avoid a much-used phrase or verbal gesture in the source, or to facilitate my desire to use that space differently, perhaps to develop more fully an exciting idea or metaphor, or to pursue a freer portrayal of what was happening at that point in the poem. This productive and liberating looseness of approach was, in my view, an enlivening and justifiable aspect of my living collaboration with Hafez. I must confess that I did stretch the "collaboration" to include adjustments that served the structural pressures of this book, taking the modest liberty of modulating the tenor of some parts of some poems to render them more consistently (or cogently) a *Slaking* or a *Thirst* poem, though I was never reckless, I believe, with the essential movement of any of Hafez's poetry.

While on the subject of accuracy and rigour, I realise that some prosodists may be perturbed to find that these eighty-one poems don't conform, in any tight sense, to the ghazal form as ordinarily described. In reassurance, let me say that many of the conventions and formal constraints that apply in the Persian do carry over into these English versions via some analogous or partially equivalent manoeuvre or prosodic device (although the degree of those equivalences vary from poem to poem). For example, in Persian, the lines in ghazals should be of identical length. I've remodelled that feature through close attention to line breaks and the overall contour of the poem, which is sometimes very precisely arranged indeed. Ghazals also commonly incorporate their author's name (or pen name) in the final verse, frequently playing on that name's meaning. Given that *Hafez* can denote one who has memorised the Qur'an, I chose to employ instead, in many of the poems here, a punning reference to the 'Reader', or, very occasionally, suitable substitutes like 'Rememberer' or 'Faithful Sun' (the latter modified from 'Sun of the Faith' – see Bell, p.21). Then there's the idea that the verses in a ghazal should each 'convey a complete thought… strung like pearls on a thread, which makes them a necklace, the value whereof lies in the value of each pearl, not in the thread' (Clarke's Preface, xiv). This is something I've borne strongly in mind throughout *Beloved*. My efforts to apply it, however, aren't exhaustive and were tempered, I'm sure, by my immersion in the Western propensity for absolute logical continuity in poetry. I could go on to elucidate and illustrate how (and how far) I endeavoured to parallel other traditional expectations relating to the ghazal, such as (say) metre, rhyme, refrain and theme; but that would be to embark upon a lengthy technical discourse of limited value to the general reader.

I should elaborate, though, on some of the goals, challenges and rewards of the thoroughly absorbing undertaking this project has been. I certainly delighted in attempting to pick up and recreate, in some way, the plurality of the Persian text (a characteristic amply demonstrated by Clarke's copious notes). I was keenly engaged, as well, with preserving all the pressure and authenticity of Hafez's sensuously material and supernal intent, content to follow closely the spirit of my primary source, as I perceived it, whilst accomplishing the most successful English poems I could. In the foreword to the 1995 edition of Gertrude Bell's versions of Hafez (see sources listed earlier), Farhad Shirzad offers little prospect of any clinching success in this respect:

> The musicality, play on words and intentional vagueness which make the poems especially attractive in the Persian, make them almost impossible for the translator.

I admit that I've found it rare for any English rendition of Hafez to convey, simultaneously, the full intensity, humanity and subtle directness of his devotion to beauty and divinity, the outright ferment and wonderment, his seriously generous exuberance and untrammelled despair, along with the linguistic grace and sonority, the easy wordplay and invitation to multiple interpretation. To redress such shortcomings may seem a near-futile exertion; but striving for the articulation, in English, of the abovementioned qualities, as realised in the Persian, was utterly invigorating and a chief aim of these translations, in spite of my extreme inexperience in the source language.

Going further into Shirzad's notion of 'intentional vagueness', one of the most pleasingly complicating facets of Hafez's work is how his references can so often be understood in a composite manner. Numerous phrases of his are elaborate puns that can be taken, suggestively, in a variety of ways, while his named persons may, at times, implicate more than a single character. Accordingly, I refrain, wherever I can, from fossilising (through my own or any scholarly investigation) the likely identities (as far as these can be unravelled or intuited) of Hafez's addressees and subjects. In addition, I may take a character or reference that appears relatively precise and, in the spirit of multiplicity, transmute it into a suitably many-faced archetype or metaphor. The 'Beloved' provides a notably recurrent example of Hafez's layering of identity. Indeed, it's not unreasonable to claim that this epithet, so regularly used by him, embodies a varying and indeterminate amalgam of devotional elements which include: Shakh-i-nabat ('branch of sugarcane': the actual and very beautiful young woman with whom Hafez so famously fell in love, but who also came to represent his muse, a manifestation of celestial loveliness walking the earth); the Perfect Master (a God-realised soul, probably in the abstract, but in the living form, too, of Hafez's own spiritual teacher, Attar); and, ultimately, the ultimate mystery of God. This indeterminacy in Hafez is facilitated by the genderlessness of the Persian language and the inherently delicious expressiveness, the sheer variety of phrasing, available to its poets. Hafez's blending of his earthly muse with the divine Beloved strikes one as a rich fusion rather than mere confusion; but it is a richness that resists easy paraphrase. Interpretative fuzziness is, of course, a built-in problem in all translation; but it's especially acute in this case. It's no surprise, then, that so many English versions of Hafez have struggled to retain a total and wholly convincing responsiveness to the original. I'm therefore sanguine about the legitimacy of having chosen a fairly open rendering of the originals for *Beloved* – especially as it seems quite plausible to suppose that Hafez himself would have approved.

Some readers might feel that not all vagueness is good vagueness, and that I could have provided a glossary (as some translators of Hafez do) explaining the credible meanings of the various symbolic terms used repeatedly in the Persian, such as: sun, moon and sky; the cup, wine and tavern; the bulbul and the rose; the field and the garden; cypress and Judas tree; the Beloved's hair, curls, lip, brow, cheek, "down" and mole. I was tempted to do so, but felt that this would have led to a very different kind of reading experience for these translations, one that would encourage flitting between poem and gloss in ways that narrow and freeze the scope and fluidity of the reader's own fathoming. I wanted Hafez's complexes of symbolic meaning to emerge in their own way, more mysteriously, through the poems themselves. For similar reasons, I've also kept the footnotes to a downright minimum.

There are a few typographical matters I might have discussed in full; I shall, instead, be brief. Some readers will note, for instance, that my capitalisations aren't consistently applied (e.g., 'tavern'/ 'Tavern'). This is partly because their excessive use would congest the text, and partly to undermine any assumption in the reader that only capitalised items can denote heavenly or Godly metaphor. The penchant in this book for hyphenation and hyphenated forms ('wine-cup', 'prayer-mat', 'musk-pod', and so on) is in slight measure my own, but is mostly a reflection of Clarke's overall style. It also lends the poetry, one could say, an apposite whiff of antiquity. More worryingly, perhaps, I've excluded diacritics from the text; but this was important in simplifying the look and the typesetting of the book, and is, in any case, a practice that isn't altogether unknown elsewhere. Also, I should add that the concrete shapes into which so many of these poems organically grew are most accurately reproduced, in their intricate detail, in Times New Roman.

Finally, wherever I do (infrequently) use Persian names, I've tended to follow Clarke's spellings (unless a hugely familiar historical personage is involved, where I've preferred the name's common English form). One exception, however, is my choice of *Hafez* over *Hafiz*. I favour this for a number of reasons, not least the assertion (again, in Shirzad's foreword to Bell's translations) that it represents 'a more contemporary English spelling'. That striving for the up-to-date isn't out of place here. For all his cult status as an ancient classic, I find just about everything in Hafez to be profoundly and refreshingly relevant to the violent sleepwalking that characterises much of our current human crisis. Having now spent real time with Hafez, I've unquestionably sensed in myself not only a galvanisation in my poetic practice but also, crucially, a recalibration in my "modern" thinking and feeling on life. That's an alchemy I don't take for granted. Whether or not Hafez's works were actually consulted by Queen Victoria in times of need, and way beyond the long-standing use of his poems as oracle in the Persian-speaking world, it's clear that his impact on culture and consciousness has been – and will continue to be – deep and enduring. Hafez maintains his potency for each passing generation, both publicly and privately, because the poet's sensibility maps itself out on the timeless canvas of the soul's necessary migration. So, yes, I expect that the (probably less usual) spelling 'Hafez' might draw from some readers a smilingly quizzical or searching frown. If it does, I'd consider that in-the-moment reaction an entirely appropriate (if unconscious) means of self-initiation into my idiosyncratic presentation of a sublimely skilled and eternally soul-affirming poet.

MARIO PETRUCCI

SOURCE POEMS

The most important source for this book was the prose text supplied in *The Divan-i-Hafiz*, translated by Lieut.-Col. H. Wilberforce Clarke (Calcutta, 1891). Clarke's Preface explains how he worked 'from the Persian text, edited by Major H.S. Jarrett, and published, under the auspices of the Government of India, in 1881 at Calcutta'. He also utilised various 'lithographed copies' with 'copious notes (in Persian)' that were available at that time in the bazaars of major Indian cities; in all such copies, he found the poems 'arranged in the same order, but not with the same paging'. For those wishing to locate the original texts, or who are curious to study the many notes supporting them, I supply (below) Clarke's two reference numbers: 'the un-bracketed number refers to Jarrett's Persian text, and the bracketed, to the bazar Persian text' (Clarke's Preface, vi). For certain poems in Clarke, however, the 'bazar' number is not present.

The Thirst

Beloved 1	*1 (1)*	Beloved 14	*169 (125)*
Beloved 2	*9 (12)*	Beloved 15	*179 (222)*
Beloved 3	*11 (11)*	Beloved 16	*191 (147)*
Beloved 4	*12 (5)*	Beloved 17	*194 (234)*
Beloved 5	*16 (18)*	Beloved 18	*227 (-no number given-)*
Beloved 6	*17 (17)*	Beloved 19	*228 (134)*
Beloved 7	*31 (74)*	Beloved 20	*244 (121)*
Beloved 8	*38 (96)*	Beloved 21	*268 (-no number given-)*
Beloved 9	*45 (37)*	Beloved 22	*284 (291)*
Beloved 10	*56 (53)*	Beloved 23	*323 (317)*
Beloved 11	*95 (111)*	Beloved 24	*325 (336)*
Beloved 12	*111 (114)*	Beloved 25	*340 (341)*
Beloved 13	*117 (132)*	Beloved 26	*347 (347)*

A note on footnotes

Where the footnote to a poem refers to 'Clarke' or 'Bell', the full details for those sources are listed in my Preface.

*

'Who's there?'

The lover answers: 'Me.'

'Go away. There's no room inside for the two of us.'

The lover knocks again. The voice once more demands: 'Who's there?'

The lover answers, 'It is You.'

'Come,' says the voice. 'I am within.'

RUMI

(text adapted by Mario Petrucci)

*

BELOVED

81 poems from Hafez

THE THIRST

1

O wine-bearer! When first I drank from your bowl
all Love seemed easy. How heavily now head and heart dissolve.

Night's nape brought blood's bouquet, a musk of such promise
dawn ends – dispatching curls of darkness without so much as a kiss.

Imbue this place of prayer, my heart, with heart-wine. At his cross
the Wise One too stood, knew this steep incline through stations of loss.

How to commit to holy pleasure or to ease when any witless after-birth
moment can intervene to blow out the just-lit candles with final breath?

This pitched night, its incoming swell, that whirlpool – death – reaching…
Do the already dead guess how lightly we living tread their beach?

It brought me only poor reputation to run my shore shoeless to God and wine.
Why should secret love be so silenced on such great assemblies of wind?

Reader, if you desire flight on diaphanous wings into brightest clearest Worth,
be attentive to sky. And once you spy your target, kick forever away from earth.

2

Zephyr – whisper to that velvet fawn, my God,
how I wander alone upon crag, along desert sand.

His honey-sellers live well, making no enquiry
of me, that parrot who squawks among His bees.

Bee-keepers, when you glug mead, chanting hymns,
think of me confusedly measuring storm with stub-wings.

You velvet roses, do your petals soar too high in flight
to bother with the honest struggle of His nightingale?

Or does each pretty squall keep visionaries – those wise
buds of bird – looking up, trapped before they blossom into sky?

Why do worldly beauties lack that pallor of fidelity –
the blackened eyes, each moon-face seen through straight trees?

How can womanly beauty be slack, other than in this respect:
when that bird fluttering within from heavenly Love deflects?

So, make of companions and the graces of fortune a form
of gratitude: lift a glass to the homing bird grounded on the plain.

Let skies, then, clear to my utterance in the Highest –
let Venus sing these humble words to raise the dancing Christ.

3

Who, to the Sultan's court, will deliver this prayer:
Why not give a beggar succour in gratitude for power?

From keen-eyed desire – that demonic nature – I hide in grace.
Can Light, with goodness undivided, bend Itself to us?

Fullest Moon, Your enkindled face illuminates beyond reach!
No one in night can be removed from Your lightest touch.

Beloved. Truest! To the steady Moon, what is Earth's restless love?
That silver face, from looming shelter of cypress, draws my heart's dove.

Through twilight years I believed that some loving, ceaseless Breath
would one day choose to release – only me – with its kiss.

Your very eyelash is an arrowhead aimed at humanity, at death.
Yes, You will one day spill me. I beg, Beloved – do not miss.

Or God, do You possess a dark side: a wide and empty eye that set me
here obscure as flesh, that sees this marked heart as mere target?

Teacher, in the name of Love, give your earliest-rising pupil the cup.
Let that be our reward – a kind of living, mutual dawn – my waking up.

Dense with being apart, this heart fills – fills again with blood's heat.
What could I be if, for an instant, it acquired Your beat?

4

That simple action, right by God: where is it? And I – without it?
What path etched on the world cannot lead from one nightfall to the next?

Separate from myself, I am far from All: lend no traction to good or wrong.
Deaf to the roadside's Holy bird, even to the evangelist guitar, I limp on.

In temples, I grew guilt-thin. How wearying, to carry hypocrisy's heavy quilt.
Circling dervish, extinguishing self, where may I glimpse you? Where is it –

God's wine? Our union, with morning, is a drunken memory. My vessel: dry.
Those strong advances – now a simper. The wise chastisements – gone. Why?

Friend, love-luminous, You show nothing to the graceless camps of the enemy.
They are blown lamps – so let me see that. Sun's waxing face: why that disguise?

The dust from His sandals, His soul's sweepings, are kohl for my blinking eyes.
Where are we going? Command me. From here – to where? Where – exactly?

Yes, a chin's bittersweet dimple took me in. That Eden-apple opened a pit.
Raw heart – why did you flurry into it? Instead of soaring, you flit.

Reader, if you seek here simplistic release or patience – read deeper.
Release – is what? Patience – what? As for sleep – you know where that leads.

5

O Sultan, my Sultan! – have pity on a meagre outsider. He replied:
Outside? Who put you outside your own heart? Are you a dog to God?

I said: Then why not let me in? *Ah – imposition is no door*, He said.
I saw how delicately is poised Perfection at its threshold with the human.

Why would nuanced Consciousness, in repose on its heavenly couch, bed
down instead among worldly spines or fill His pillow with mortal bone?

You: whose tresses snag souls as trees unnumbered birds have done.
You: whose face is the sun, the mole on Your cheek a transiting Venus.

That corona of light so fine around Your face – a down of brightness.
In His cosmic gallery, how could such a God not hang such a Sun?

See how Your moon blushes with dawn to reflect Your hidden glow.
Watch the rose petal of Judas fall strangely into the wild cup of Rose.

I said: Your lovely hair, so dark it flecks with light – let me nest
entwined there. In the morning: a single speckled egg. No regret.

I said again: Why rush to set below the horizon in blushed hue,
in separation? Moon! Why flay the one who seeks to see You?

He said: *Watcher – see how the child, feeling small, cranes in awe
for the astonished face of moon, brought close because it is so far.*

Morning. Cloud upon cloud, parts petalled light. Sun: so thinly veiled,
red-lipped, You depart the bridal tent. Friends – lift cups to that Face!

The worldly man opens his blood like a tulip. That spot within: blackly held.
The dew freezes upon him – he dies. Lift cups instead to intoxicant space!

As blades of grass, the holy hordes advance. From them – a lasting breeze.
Bouquets of Paradise rise with their dust. Please, let me breathe that draught!

Within this grass is set a rosebush, greened in prayer. First, a single jewel;
then a crown. Ruby each cup to a brimming flower! Pour coolest wine.

But heart and mind shut their tavern. Once more, no liquid forgiveness.
Tavern-master – unbolt Your doors. Open up for holy business!

Let me in then seal all access behind me.
Lock me in. Quickly!

If any should lean in to pluck the grains from Your lip's fire, You require
that they use that salt to dress the wounds their roasting hearts desired.

Poor teachers: drink yourselves into oblivion like the student fool.
Fellow pupils – practise prudence! Be sure to follow the rules.

If you thirst for truest water, why scour riverbeds for signs?
Here sounds the eternal chord of the harp. Here, the Wine.

Wise Reason, wishing for sharper spirit on your tongue:
sip whispers from the claret lips of your Beloved One.

Remember, smooth-cheeked angels hide terrible teeth
: while roses bloom, consume their blood-wine truth.

Reader: don't give in to dust. Each cloud must lift.
Love Love to one day look on His face and live.

Ah Breath – whether you brush the stones of the Holy Lands
or comb the tree-heads there – rush here with their perfume.

Upon my one soul, it is far better to let fly this blood-bond
and die than miss any word, a single letter, from the Groom.

Air, if your insinuations find no means, if every door is sealed,
at least accost from His stair some dust: collyrium to help me see.

Where now that intent, urgent Self, to merge? Lost. Beggarly.
Asleep, might I yet sense some contour, a shadow of Your outline?

I am trembled willow. A pine-cone blown against by God's Name.
A cone that can grow the Tree entire – this is the form of the heart.

I was bought by Him with no more than a sand-grain, a mote of light;
yet I would refuse all Persia in exchange for one strand of His thought.

Reader: what use? – to be released from the binds and vows of holy Pain
only to find yourself re-bound, awaiting all over – His pleasure – again.

8

Within your seductive black-lashed Eye – something sleeps.
Your dashed and tumbled rockslide-Hair hides something deep.

I pray – and your Smile runs something sweet as nipple-milk
when I say: *Fresh water-honey from your salt-pan Lips, I drink.*

That Mouth is a spring welling far more than what I lack: yet
at its rim that apple of your Chin – its tiny pit – distracts.

Live always! Your crossbow brow makes every Eyelash sly
as bolts about to go. Some undying wish in me says: let fly!

Heart – you broke and break again seeing the empty Bed.
Be keen in your lamentation – and Something shall be heard.

In hushed night, from your Hills, arose a frost – it brushed
the collar of my rose. White petals, I spilled. Nothing was lost.

Reader: there's nothing to gain in making public such weeping:
though, from the tear wept there, the eye does keep something.

9

Beside His cheek, darkly, hang those worldly locks. Suspended on a hair:
hearts by thousands. From a thousand sages, that loveliest cheek hides.

So that souls would merge with His fragrant breeze, He sent out on widest
air an urgent, perfumed note. Yet when we dance to the Door: no one there.

Beloved had me glimpse – a Brow: crescent moon that shed a light so proud
it unsettled me. The heavens shifted – subtly – He set again behind a cloud.

The glories of destiny pour, for the desiring cup, a love of rainbowed hues:
see – how He paints His arc in the essential heart, as though it were open blue.

God: by what mystery did the Vessel – waters within gurgling sweetly, swan
neck swooned up to heaven – turn to blood and flood silence into the room?

In the heart of the holy ceremony, what struck note brought the ecstatic pressure
to a stillness where either harp or barking door give the listener equal pleasure?

The master Magician sees this world as a temporary sphere of tricks, then
becomes clear: brings to a close his student assembly and never talks again.

Reader: if, without any room for love, with hands unwashed, you still desire
the Bride – walk yourself as if naked to the Father's house in pilgrim attire.

10

My moon vacated the city this week – to my eyes, it seems a year.
Have you seen, from your own nights, how darkly separation glares?

Her cheek gave such holy light, I saw my moon-eye there: my own
weak pupil, suspended in reflection. I thought it her moon-mole.

From that sky-hung lip, as nursing-milk, her light is dripping-sweet:
and yet, in every glance, the eye-lashed rays rain down to annihilate.

Moon: gratefully, our citizens point as you guide them on our streets:
but strangers stand in wonder at the disinterest when you illuminate.

Because of you, I am certain now of the indivisible atom: the proof
lies in those ambrosia infinitesimals, the fresh integral, of your mouth.

In loving company, Fate and Destiny brought word – that you would
pass us by. Please don't make it otherwise: the omen must be good.

Through what skill does that grievous author of mountainous separation
draw this splintered poet whose body, weeping, is a fibre from his pen?

Vintner – tread my vine entire, oblivious, into wine.
Unstoppable dancer! Chance upon me, break me down.

You ask: *When shall you, as solitary grape, desist?* In a rush,
even as You make this sweet request, I'm eager for the must.

Or am I the drunk unseemly as empty bottles, whom none attends?
If only Your steward would pour, serenely downwards I'd ascend.

As the groom to his bride, Time strides to Doom with splayed arms.
I am sand in their hourglass, for lack of Your greyest sideways glance.

You say: *My lips that draw blood are also a pitcher brimming elixir.*
Either way – be it dread kiss or tongued flood – I'll sweetly expire.

But yes, how daintily You tread. Toes unstained, no sloe-eyed evil
alights on Your frame. I swell one hope: as a grape Underfoot, to go.

Winemaster, if I'm never to glut at your private vat, grant me this wish:
as a dewdrop sensing its ocean, let me once taste You and be finished.

Light-giving lamp, how right it is that fireflies should swarm to you:
as a jewel to be clamped in its crown, each spark flits to your flame.

Your wine-filled eyes bring bustling Turkey to line our streets. To view
how your hair slides from a shoulder, our borders come running headlong.

In a mood of mercy, that white of your cheek outshines the noonday sun:
in wrath, your mane is more intensely black than starless, moonless night.

This is my scourge: that I yearn for you and yet must remain ever apart.
Even my most urgent pangs force no remedy; I am doubtful of any cure.

Your perfect mouth pouts, and makes permanent a Godly gush of purity.
Those lips of sugarcane outstrip in sweetness lakes of Egyptian honey.

Upon my soul! Are you so diamond-hearted that you'd happily grind
this single crystal of blood, suspended frozen and fragile in my breast?

One strand from your head can tether the most muscular waist, or bind
the leviathan hard to its shore, or raise a great city's domes to free air.

Fresh with currents of the Perfect Master, your curls ripple everywhere.
Your height is cypress, your waist a hair, your nape of burnished ivory.

Yet, into this brain, fell a desire – as a bird alighting to roost in its tree.
By your door, in the corner of devotion, I serve the dust of your floor.

13

From darkest blood, this bulbul sang to father a rose: but
jealously the wind wound it in thorns, punctured the heart.

Delirious with the promise of sugar, this parrot squawked –
but saw the sweet grains lost, blown to the floor by a squall.

Memory's a flame, cool in the pupil – an apple, unconsumed,
its glossy burden hung within. All will pass, my son, too soon.

Master of caravans: you saw my sad bundle slip into sand. Aid me
– some kindness at least might stall the loss on this longest journey.

Don't deplore the kneaded face laid with dust, these streaming eyes;
this frame in clay and straw is a palace devised by the sky's blue dome.

In its sphere, the moon loosed envious arrows: made my sun disappear.
See, too, how the stony tomb borrows its lunar complexion from there.

Like a king, careless at chess, I neglected to castle: now my board turns
black. Time, I ignore your weeping clock. The game ends. My line ends.

'Hafiz wrote this ode on the death of his son.' (Clarke, p.244)

14

If I pursue You, You turn on me with an almighty
fuss – if I sit down again, You angrily stand up.

On the road, if my passion causes me to flop at
Your feet, Your gust carries the dust off without me.

Yet, if I try a kiss unrequited, some half-way mouth,
then sherbet chastisements pour from Your pout.

The dunes of love, with their crests and slacks, entrap:
where is the desert lion brave enough to enter all that?

If Your deceit lies in the eye of beholders, I'm lost
nonetheless: Your glance turns any reputation to rust.

I try to speak, asking: *Why are You so promiscuous?*
Your answer is to marry, in me, my blood and tears.

Reader: for a long life, be longsuffering – then see
how roundly this cosmos lends itself to trickery.

Let's lay these insistent heads on surrender's block:
to resist is to be on your deathbed tilting at clocks.

15

Beloved: when the lustre of Your cheek sheens the wine-cup, even that knowing Wine-lover can fall from laughter into a cheap need to drain it.

This world is a jewel reflecting Your image: those loveliest features play over its facets, until our tapestry of living figures can unpick the illusion.

If those souls kick like a compass, ever gaining no ground through mere revolution, what can be done? Oh: that impassive round of Time's circle!

Lord: You glimpsed me, remember, gliding through cloisters? That game is up. Now I strain for Your cup-bearer's soaking face, the brimming rim.

It's proper to dance, openly, beneath this fresh Blade of longing: its happy stroke makes a fabled death.

This leap from dogma to tavern was never my doing: I was thrust into wine, from behind, by the Beginningless Covenant.

True Love is jealous: it stumped to pure silence the tongues of Great Ones. How can it entrust to such humdrum lips its secretive service of yearning?

Yes, each instant washes my Master, ash-warm, through my chest – I am that worthy one flashed blissfully to nothing.

Prisoner in Your dimpled chin, I shinned that rope of locks, only to find Your curls a subtler flock of snares.

On that Beginningless Morning, the Perfect One slipped radiant from mist, illuminating our human features with resplendence we only, at best, reflect.

What sensual wine – or crass love, so various – indeed reflects, is a clouded semblance of the true face of the Wine-bearer pouring into hearts and minds.

Holy climbers, seeing singly, achieve the summit; with troubled eye, bound by reason and desire, the oily one slides to the pit. World sees world double.

Ah, I was up among the Sufis once: those glowing wine-lovers who play well the drunken glance – until my wasted heart, legless with height-sickness, fell.

16

My tears, I've begun to fear, will release this urgency to roam
the world unveiled: one step it is, from sealed letter to rumour.

They say that the river's pebbles, if patient, merge to wild ruby:
but the crude stone must be polished and set in the liver's blood.

I've lost patience with the lusty superiority of hypocrites. God
forbid that a reverence for beggary should emerge to swell heads.

Yet, Your look has something of the haughtiness of cypress in it
– in its shade, our stump thumbs barely hook into Your bark belt.

Blind in the forest, I launched prayerful arrows along every arc –
perhaps one of these, by kind accident, will have done its work?

See: Your form, over this imperial palace, hovers as its Moon.
The dust at its gate bends worthiest heads to supplicant brooms.

Still, this Love I bear in me alchemises old flesh to fresh gold:
in Your foundry of paradises, yes, dust shall be killed into gold.

As well as blossom, every corner of our garden must burgeon
with all subtleties of Being, to please the gaze of the All-seeing.

For this, I'll go to the Wine-house weepy, clutching emptiness:
might someone there prise open this clench of grief in my chest?

Soul, rustle my story in the Heart-keeper's ear: the summer tree
puts leaf to the gust, not loosing one to air where everyone sees.

And if an awful tide should blight us, why swamp upper rooms
crying? Crawl to God, in gratitude, against greater misfortune.

Be still: pains needn't clump into suffering. Night's dark shawl
is sun's shadow. Morning's rose opens against the blackest wall.

Reader: if the Beloved tip of a curl fragrantly kisses your hand,
breathe in; your moment, exhaling, flits on the lips of the wind.

Only Love can smother the embattled head and heart: at birth,
I sucked it in with mother-milk; I shall soon rattle it out at death.

Even in the tomb, this skull will crack and lift to greet Those
feet: ah, if the tread that sifts my dust be Yours, I wish it so.

I smart for You, I said. You replied: *Grief has its ends.*
I said: Kindle me to Moonbeam. *When the clouds part*, You replied.

I began: Be my full Moon… *No*, You corrected – *Half-moon. Yin-yang.*
I wooed: Will You soon send it? You replied: *Not before I do.*

Once more I tried: See how Your avowed lovers are an epitome
of fidelity. You replied: *From their moony cheek comes poor illumination.*

I said: I'll steer my stare from vain crowds – away – right at You!
You replied: *Night-prowlers remain awake, gain entry by unexpected means.*

I spoke: Your fragrant locks made me nomad to the world – lost to its byways.
You replied: *That myrrh, delectable within you, is also your star.*

I said: This glad air I breathe, stroked by love's leaves, makes me sad enough.
You laughed: *Pleasanter is the breeze from My street corner.*

I spoke again: At Your bluff lip, that sweet drip You dangle… banishes me!
You said: *Attend Me, and your soul is beloved, cherished.*

I said: When will Your heart's heart tender me to rest?
You said: *Desist – why speak of such turbulence while heart-blood is shed?*

I insisted: Surely, You see how brief is Your flood, how long Your ebb?
You whispered: *Be still now. All grief has an end.*

18

My house became the home of an exquisite spirit
in whom – hair to toe – none could reveal any defect.

A spirit so perceptive, so comely, is born from on high:
a moon of elevated stature – a boon from the All-Wise.

My heart declared: Stay near to this rare spirit; here.
Exposed, it held little fear of the other's departure.

From embrace, this was swept by a blighting star.
What is one to do with night, when the moon stops?

Now, from my inmost being, has fallen each mystery.
Skies, too – since Time made them – let their stars drop.

Verges of water, roses, rivers of grass: these sat with me
once; but they are merely treasure that is sinking sweetly.

Time, then, became drinkable in that treasured company –
a wine to which all other moments seemed thin, tasteless.

Dawn parts Love's petals, but the bird-heart is envious:
if Death should try to steal the last whisper, I'd die first.

But heart, be excused. You're only a beggar, and it was in
realms of beauty that your companion's head was crowned.

Ah: to the aching spirit, God's treasures come from kneeling
under one star of sleeping and many heart-breaks of waking.

'This poem, Hafiz composed, some say, on the sudden death of a friend;
and others on the death of his wife.' (Clarke, p.415)

19

Perhaps it's not my fate to feel the outline of Your lips.
To Your secret shape, the hidden place, will chance admit me?

Desire kills me, and I lack the means to pierce the screen of divinity:
the screen's Keeper, steeped in perfection, won't give it to me.

For the Lips that would ready me for the life-hush, I'd extinguish me;
yet You spurn *this*: my life; and resist *that*: the opening Kiss.

The bower-breeze caressed Your soft tresses, sighed; yet this churlish
cosmos has denied me the power to unfurl a single curl.

See, how the compass-point must keep to circumference: I turn and
turn – ever kept from my centre by cardinal Time.

Love, grain by grain, in hives of quelled blood: one may accrue it –
but, all too soon, faithless Time consumes it.

I said to myself: Go to bed; dream the sweet Prize… But so deep
went my cries, I made sleep sleepless.

20

If ever I turn, in shame, from the head of Your street,
may I then be progressed to ultimate shame.

By the Master's star, a traveller must constantly redress –
side roads and bazaars give weariness no rest.

At the journey's very end: that is when we raise a holy glass.
I'll not steer stray flesh towards endless idleness.

Guide, help a heedless heart back to Love's breast:
a rider can follow the masterful Steed if caught in storms of dust.

We call one *sober*, another *drunk*, favouring parts over the whole;
but no one, at the last, knows which way they'll fall.

Mine is the caravan led by Grace: my bed awaits in the final Tent;
I know my place; but oh, the unrelenting sands within…

Reader, if you find that Fountain's rim in you, drink
its wisdom and you'll rinse, from your inner tomb, all inscription.

21

Before the merchandise and stalls, God's perchancers advertise:
All of you half-alive on the Beloved's streets – Listen! It has been

a full week since Love dried up, evaporant to her own desire. Now
watch for her quenching torch. She'll ripple down in claret and rose,

froth-crowned as if fire had just poured itself into glass. Deprived by her
of insight and reason, you see how in sleep you might both drown and burn?

Bring the sour sweet that she is, and I'll wake this soul, still sweeter, to drink.
If to infernal black she sank, even there my deepest part, with her, would sum.

That daughter is a nightwalker, bitterly tart, flushed as a drunk. Yet, lacking her,
I'm unwhole. Reader, from whatever gutter, lead her to that hushed hearth: my heart.

You are not lost. Joseph, though devoured, will return to Canaan.
Through low trees, upon each sad family of cells, dawn dapples roses.

Ah, hurt-struck heart, sorrows soften. Wait, then, before exposing ills.
Shipwrecked minds rise, bob again to surface reason, spilling excess brine.

Oh, night-sung bird, draw the canopy of thorns to shield your bones –
spring arrives before too long. The rose prince shall claim his green throne.

What firmly hides, hard in winter's bud, you may never see. Yet
keep hope fresh. Within that stilled sap, towards life, stir subtle chemistries.

If you walk this world straight in step, yet run in circles without
a guide, avoid despair. You'll intersect at last with a sure-footed teacher.

If today follows yesterday, the revolving heavens never bringing rain,
remember that wheel must reverse. Weather pain; it will pass.

When, in granite desire for the sacred house, you traverse the desert,
see how holy spines pierce you only to bring you home. Why exclaim?

Ah, the black-stone heart! When it seems, in mortal flood, your foundation
must yield, Noah himself will steer you through. To the deluge, add no tears.

Stride through fear. Fear is this world, fear that friendless road without refuge
or horizon. But roads come to an end. We are, ourselves, our bright tavern.

Apart from the Beloved, with prying eyes preying on us: this might seem
our condition. Confusion! God, causing all, sees all. Let grief unfold.

Reader: unfed in your corner, alone in black night, turn inside yourself
each leaf of that Holy Book. Recite yourself. Inner, other worlds console.

23

One lobe of Your ear… Pierced for silver,
for stone, my heart hangs there: restless, senseless, quelled.

A flame, dancing. A peerless, smokeless flicker.
Now, subtle as a noonday moon; now, stood there, open-robed.

Love surges – in fires upwardly urged, such a heat
as seethes. This sugar rises in my cauldron, writhes alarmingly.

Were I Your open robe, rightful in embrace, my heart
could slacken into peace, sit snugly in me, tight-fitting, calm.

But weeping is a wingless bird. And who would wish
the rosebush, in its budding, thornless, the beehive stingless?

Even if these living, truest bones should turn to mash,
this soul will be remembered in its lonely love for You.

Head says: *Blood and death! Blood and death!*
But heart beats: *Love and breath! That lovely neck!*

A secret: the reckless cure… my cure is a sip
from honeyed lips. Those pure lips! Your lips.

Last night, I sensed it. Suddenly, the air knew its mysteries,
said: *Nothing can conceal from you the Wineseller's secret.*

Then: *In keeping with this world, the full-blooded worker is*
bled more severely. Take yourself to yourself less strenuously.

I was given a cup. Its oval tilt of liquid was a sky – a dark, red
vault where Venus swayed and the spheres plied one word: *Drink.*

Child: you think to allay all ills with tears? There's a story most
won't touch, though I'd have it couch in you, smoother than a pearl.

With haemorrhaging heart, let laughing wine sparkle from your lips.
When inward wounds split to a ney-mouth, don't blow to wail its note.

Fail to acquaint yourself with what is hidden and you'll never earn
the heights. What angelic message can take flight in a fledgling ear?

In the body of Lovers, no part should crow how it heard this, saw that.
In Love, the self becomes an organ entire: a hawk – listening, vigilant.

In search of holy subtlety, so soft underfoot, nothing is sold or bought.
To be gold, talk on what's been assayed within – or else, speak silence.

So, pour! My drunkard hand full well is known to that lenient Vizier,
Master of forgiveness and indulgence who buries, in sand, every fault.

Your Beauty wedded this world, in every corner.
Shamed by Your moon, sun's groom blushed brighter.

Nothing can live if not in witness to Your beauteousness.
Even angels are Host-bound to look, once, upon that Face.

In the fourth heaven, sun breathes with Your radiance as if,
in itself, it were seventh earth burdened with lightless death.

The soul that never bled for its Mistress is lifeless. Flesh
unconsecrated in its Shepherd is a shorn winter sheep.

In lovesickness, with open mouth, my sad self steeps.
Your rose conserve can save – those soul-loving Lips!

But a kiss leaves no trace on the Master's shoe. Reader:
desire, our one true story, loses itself in the wind, without you.

26

Among the crowd of lovely ones, true candle, I burn constantly
for You. Among loud revellers, kept awake by sighs, I steadily burn.

Through each ungodly hour, eyes resist sleep: this sour worship of grief!
Sputtering separation, weeping wax, You could put me out with one breath.

By sorrow's shears my patient wick was cut, so that in hot, utter dissolution
I might laugh away these drops.

       Night. I am alone. Will You not send word
of togetherness? Do – or watch how a solitary candle can consume worlds.

See this blood-tint of tears, how the soft pearls start down my cheek. Each
rides the rash back of need, gallops to turn furtive Love to public lamp.

Through damp and heat, assailed, this stub of heart, guttering frail
drips, is ever ardent in desire.

      In persistence, I was mountainous.
Now, in the cauldron, my wax is purified, softened by sadness.

Dawn is dusk without You, the world unadorned. Perfection
is that candle losing itself in gas and flame, born into nothing.

Extend me, a neck of wax, up, till this dark head alights in Your lap.
Sight of Your face would enkindle my cell, dazzle this humble candle.

Without glimpse of You, morning's pale rinse brings only shallow breath;
seducer, show Yourself and I'll offer – in drooping, dropping wax – my life.

What wonder, that wicked heads can become the wick for a Love so simple.
What watery eye can ever quench that rising fire: a heart's insistent candle?

Teacher! If a flagon should come your way, across this clay sprinkle a taste.
I am Adam, dust. Evil: why fear it? All evil is shunned in enlightening dust.

Now, at sky's peak, as though air might be a mountain, let light rend itself,
burst its protective curtain. Or is sky's narrow tomb, death-dark, an end?

So, drain all you can: force it down, whatever's at hand, without remorse.
Time presses its long edge against your nape.

                                          Great cypress! Grace my dust
with Your root. I trust that same root, when I at last depart, will consolidate.

To denizens of hell, of heaven, every woman, man – anyone, even angels – say:
All may know Oneness, but step from the path. Keep to Love's well-worn ways.

That geometer of air made world a hive of reason: up-down, front-back, side to
side. There, in six-cornered cells, heads imperial, we are stung flightless – die.

Reason is tongue-tied by grapes' fluent Daughter. Let vines burgeon, prosper
to be savoured at the end of days.

I was content once, idler on my sure way to the wine-house. But, if pure,
a heart is consoled by the purer heart's prayer – by its own prayer. Pray.

28

Your slow shape, the way You move, blows hearts to chaff.
To each: Your *No*. A loving planet tilts towards You, jilted.

Sometimes, in separation, I release a sigh – almost a laugh.
Othertimes, You draw the arrow from my heart's dark quiver.

How to explain, to beasts that lie in wait, the ruby of those Lips?
The worldly adore dull rainbows, quip ignorance at purer hues.

Somewhere, Your beauty increases. Moon glares, but is no match:
moon is extinguishable, exhausts itself; must wane as well as wax.

Heart lost, soul relinquished – again. Am I Your only dwelling
for gloom? I'm bankrupt. Why not send the tax collector as well?

Reader: if I ever set toe or fingertip in God's walled enclosure,
I'll grip, for holy hell, the Beloved hem – let go of this world.

29

Your morning is that broad forehead lifting the horizon, laughing with mending
Light – I am a candle on dawn's table. Smile through my window: I'll surrender.

Your tress whets me for Love to my innermost fibre. Our world may be vanishing,
yet my tomb, nonetheless, will darken with violets, close-pressed, nodding assent.

I arrive at Hope's threshold, opening my sight to be received; but You are that host
who refuses the guest.

                Grief – stacked within me, your crowded clouds brood over
pardon. Through worst days, unbefriended, your multiplying storms restlessly nest.

I'm slave to what I see: perception forbidden to pluck, from its eye, that dark apple;
yet, for all its blackness, eye's heart can't help but drip dew when I tell my troubles.

The splendid Angel bestows treasure from every angle.
                                    No one, it seems, knows.

If, across my benighted slab, the scented body of my Love should pass, like smoke,
this festering marrow will re-ignite, split the shroud, make my narrow grave a stove.

The veil between me and Beloved reality is this dust body.
In death, breath racing, I'll part at last, as if I were vapour.

I've heard in myself freer songs than from the bodily cage.
Eden's rose-beds will assuage me: I'm a bird of that temper.

Nothing material, no fact, traces back to why we were put here
or the *ergo*-urge before that. Sad regret only saps that purpose.

In this arena of time and space, how may I complete a circuit
as inconstant dust, planked shut, among competing elements?

My place is that natural theatre of angels. Why must I wait
down here, caught between worldly ghosts and inebriates?

Don't gawp, then, if this inner heart pours out pure musk.
I'm of that ilk. I share the fate of the musk-deer of China.

I quicken, flare, my face a twist of flame rising from its taper.
I try to insist on being elated; but, deeper in, I melt, evaporate.

I resist, believing one may relieve oneself of oneself. Body is
an eclipse – slip behind yourself, until the only light is God's.

The Tavern door creaks open a crack: will that splinter of light slit my heart?
I slanted my shadow down the well-lit path – but where to sit and discern?

I've nothing left for journeying. My herd of cross-purposes stalls at
the pass. I pause by that Door, spurred by a promise of liquid alms.

Let trickling tears grow, swell into weirs russet with blood, fan
over sand in harmless flows to lick and lap that flawless foot.

May heart be proofed against the blackening, bitter flood if,
in the violence of need, its tidal din, I brim with grievance.

To bleed, on Love's parchment, the mysterious mark,
must I not darken my quill in the pupil of Your eye?

My heart and soul come to You, hand in hand, lacking
favour. Your quelled smile says: *There might be a way…*

Apart from its flock, heart flies off, prey to any fragrant swirl. I
prefer to home along Your night perfume to settle in curls of myrrh.

Ah, only joyous hearts leave room for genuine grief towards the Lover.
So, I wish for gloom, for bliss, each serving the other as bride and groom.

Reader, did I sit so long beside the college door, no one could tell us apart?
The Tavern door, a crack, creaks open – a splinter of light to slit my heart.

If chance could walk me, once again, to the Perfect Master's tavern,
I'd scatter all the pious gains of prayer-mat and mantle, purposely lose them.

If, today, I forged a bright ring in penance – to sound, as the ascetic
does, one sad note – still, tomorrow's wine-house door wouldn't open to it.

If I were blessed – as the moth is – with flights of true carelessness,
I'd flutter surely towards that shimmering Face, into its soft drop of light.

If, since my harp's untuned, there's no string in me You can play,
at least, as though I were a flute, cherish me – breathe me into harmony.

I could solicit angelic forms over Yours: what a lapse, how unshapely,
to split myself thus.

        Heart liquefied inside me to blood: I hide the fact.
Since that, my newest consolation has been grief's honed blade.

My ribs never released their small red bird so passionate for You:
yet, in my eyes' wet verges, half-submerged, its secret song was heard.

I flew from body, rid myself of my cage of bones; but even air, ever open,
is just another kind of prison for those who can only fear God's talons.

Beloved: if each hair on this head were itself a head, I'd amass the fleeting
multitude of myself, as if You'd let fall impossible tresses, at Your feet.

Beloved, whenever my inner eye put pen to thought, I forever traced
Your cheek – though I have never seen Your face, or heard You close.

I saw myself as a Lord; now, to be in Your service would be promotion.
The will for realms swelled in me, then. Bent knees make a surer throne.

In my alacrity to seek You out, I exceed any steed of the northerly breezes;
but I can only glimpse Your form, far off, trailing dust like a galloping tree.

This hand, darkly entwined in Your locks through night, never closed its fist
on any strand that might brighten the day. Your round mouth, I never kissed.

At that deep eye, that enticing nape, I startled in myself like a deer in its copse,
shunning thereafter both woman and man.

                                        My eyes, desiring Your wild fountain,
juggled tears: these bought grace from lips I'd sip and swig, until this bankruptcy.

                        You hunted me once. How those arrowed glances quickened me!
Now I plough dust at the end of Your street, dragging carts over-heaped with pain.

Ah – dawn. Won't you stir? Send me a smear of pollen from the Beloved garden
to fertilise my bumbling blood. I smell incoming rains from wounded mountains.

How well I knew that scent passing overhead: an intense essence of rose-beds my
hurt tried to open to, splitting this green heart all through as though it were a bud.

I swear – by the rain-dark dirt at Your feet, by the dry glint alive in these eyes –
I never saw a radiant look, on any face, that wasn't alight with Your likeness.

One glance in my direction, and immediate agonies crumple me.
Then I catch Your look – and again I stretch towards You, abruptly.

What You secrete, deep within, evades me. You won't stride out to
cure me, never inquire into how I fare. Have You even an idea of me?

Riding past, You bump any stumbler into sand. Cast a look over that fast
-moving shoulder, dismount just once – I'll be glad dust along Your Path.

I'll forever keep this hand to Your cloak. Even when death exacts its due,
approach my grave and those sleeping grains will rear up, grope for You.

This love I hold is anguish, a labour of lack. How much longer, life?
You accept these breathless, reckless blasts – yet leave me breath?

That night when I groomed jet locks to extract my heart, Your trove
of cheek became a cup: I found my fill from lips bejewelled with Love.

Yes: I drew You in, sharply, closer than breath or dagger, heart lost among
densely wisping strands. The rest of me followed, abandoned in a final kiss.

                                        You left, without me, for greener plains.
My blood-rust rains came in gouts to gouge and darken their yellow dunes.

Be kind: insist on death, instead, with those who wish You ill. Be sun
to me, an instant, and I'll not fear foe's dead breath, nor coldest hell.

Oh, for one deep-crimson draught of Love – or to glimpse those whose gibbous
brows reflect a little. Mind seeks denial: how to leave behind the external?

Each who senses the Beloved shape keeps, beneath gilt garments, a noose
of prayer: their longer hands, so short-sleeved, seem to reach higher than most.

These don't bend to plenty, cramming coffers with either world. They glean.
Such is the knowingness of Love's beggar, the dignity of the devotee.

The Friend won't lean in to unknot the frown from the frowning brow. See
how a head can wrinkle a heart – or cow an infant grace into need.

Who hears, in any public place, a single vowel of Belovedness?
Even in the society of seekers, close-seated, I sniff some falsity of breath.

To be free of base desire, allow yourself to be bound securely
in Love's tower. That is the future for those who look up, not around.

Dear: draw Your cloth, damp with Love, across my mirror. Clear
my dust. Clarify the image of Your lamp, right here.

My sky grew green with holy nature, wider than vision. Its newly sickle moon
made a flag. Beneath, pondering that Day of Reaping, the field of me lay open.

I said: *My fortune – you've been caught in slumber by the dawn!*
The answer came: *What is past ought not to be turned to doom.*

In purity, relieved of flesh, like the very Messiah, each must rise
to yet higher skies, absorbed into the sun itself – that Sun one is.

Each night's a thief, moon its vagrant accomplice: dark will murder
worldly powers, dissolve away the greatest kings, crown and girdle.

I tell sky: *You boast of your adornments – yet I can't trust what you do or give.*
Down here, in Love's harvest, moon's halo buys a barleycorn, the Pleiades two.

An earlobe sags with rubies, gold: what good is that ring, if the ear
itself is dull to its counsel? Hear this. Youth is the shortest spring.

Beloved: evil balks at Your delectable mole. Sky has moon and sun
as birthmarks – but, on beauty's chessboard, Your black pawn wins.

Heart is a holy field, blessed by a sun that works for greenness. I must trouble
myself to sow, in faith, in myself – or come, yellow-faced, to a yield of stubble.

Like the tambourine in this circle I'm in, ring within ring, my horizon
sits in Time. Though beaten, I cannot leave; I must become the music.

Hypocrisy is an unclean flame, blackening religion's plots – deceit is that slick
breeze, blowing it through. What blame, Truth? I must defrock Ego; move on.

At dawn I sought a garden, to pick a rose.
A nightingale took fright, all at once, close.

I was that bird – lover of the bloom, entangled
in thorns. How that tiny flute, forlorn, rang out.

Now, through long moments, I stroll in that garden.
I ponder the songbird, ever wasting under its fat bud.

Rose cannot do without thorn; nightingale, in pain, is
drawn to the two. Can blossom or bird know otherwise?

That bird pressed its cry onto my heart, as if upon a scarlet
seal of wax – I'm impatient to break it, to read its secret letter.

In this garden, there's always a rose in bloom; but also that shock
of thorn. Fingertips that pick must bulge blood buds – rose insists.

Reader: be on guard. This world of flitting brains, of clipped feathers,
is a mesh of flaws, a bush sharp with hardship. Its consummation: never.

Cup-bearer: if wine is Your interest,
to serve us nothing else would be fine.

Prayer-mats, those holier-than-thou robes,
can go: sell them off for a measure of Love.

Aroused by the vine, a heart can't sleep as long
as blood's rose nightly howls: *Ever-Living Life!*

You sorrowful: right yourselves with Love's
remedy. You fiendish: forget both worlds.

Bleeding in its mystery, my heart heard:
a far strum calling; a nearby flute keening.

An old one, in Love's poverty, purely empty,
opens a palm, and outweighs every cave of gold.

You, so fair indeed: enter as Sultan. May You arrive
trailing whole tribes, nations entire, like sprawls of hair.

Every face will turn to that Face, cheeks on fire, beaded
with dews of modesty – all one in divine perspiration.

How long, this separation? When a broken soul
has spoken, honestly, must You break again?

Wine-bearer, have I fallen for the cup over its wine? I've admired, overly,
the green casing of the rose – split that bud with blossom, with lustrous red.

Desire for One so fully faced is how dust must cleave to mystery. Minstrel:
sing, until moon drops its veil. Cup-bearer: it's the very Vine you carry!

May I bend with grieving, be smoothed to fit the Lover's grip: become
a door-ring, true for opening, shaped for that one Door, not any other.

Again, I have made a friend of hopefulness: the two of us wish to see
Your face. But manifestations can be distractions when one calls in vain.

Awaiting Your look, I'm wasting to a petalless posy; less: a wordless question.
Ah, to set that jewel of Your mouth in the base metal of mine. The idea thins…

It's not for this world to witness You unveiled: so, why try to gain a glimpse?
Heart knows no eye can contain that Sun; but craves its warmth nonetheless.

Why bloody fingers, hotly straining, scrabbling in dust for the wine-cup
that never gave up even a spot of water?

      Heart: you slaughter yourself among fanciful images.
Was anyone ever saved by that far glitter of mirage?

I am nothing. A thousand strenuousnesses – still nothing. I'm
dry. I see: You may never be impassioned wine to my empty vessel.

Could You try, one time, to pass by my mournful hut? Why not slip in,
just once – a consoling shade cast by moonlight, sloped along the wall?

I was a sentinel, a wakeful lamp that kept remembering: I was never
snuffed out. I hoped we might burn together.

                                      I slept – had visions.
An end to division, to tears in cascade. You, returned, cradling me.

But Your mouth is cornelian, cut to bloody hearts. Though the agony
bending me could rouse a nation, let it remain in the dark, a mystery.

If the great and gorgeous should condescend, suddenly, easily,
to their minions, still, in this blind mess, I'd work only for You.

If You could, become a slender hind haunting the trees, a gleaming
moment… Do this, and I'd hunt even the canopy's shifting sunbeams.

Inwardly, outwardly, with every Word, You promised three kisses to my
two lips. Give – or be the One in silent debt.

                                    I hear there's a deep, steep valley
where Love offers the lover its hand. Beloved, did You forget to seek mine?

Me, guardian over the coffers of Your city? This weeping ear of barley?
Perhaps, out of godly generosity, You'll reap me – this nothing I am.

THE SLAKING

This desiring head I dare place upon the pillow of God's bed.
Whether dream or nightmare hovers there – it is all Beloved.

I hold my mirror to Her sleeping face: that white sun; the cool, full-
bright moon of Her – still, by comparison, these reflections are dull.

How hearts seize themselves against spring! As the first bud of rose,
reddening, we weld our petals shut. But in that breeze – what news?

In inner taverns, drunkards abound. Unalone, I gulp that richer world,
ravaged by thirst, where great works are the patina on the wine-pitcher.

Your long comb combed Your hair to make of air ambergris – this
I know. Now breeze is civet. Even dust lifts to me scented lips.

Your tears are what the expressive rose sprinkles on lawns.
Each cypress towering over riverbank: there in Your form.

To translate Your loving whispers, even poetry is mute.
That split tongue of reed lies enfeebled in its instrument.

Exposed to grace, fixed in need, my heart carries Your likeness.
Soon, by that light-pressed imprint, Your truest Face I'll glimpse.

My heart, its own torched flower, grows beyond time to all Light has:
through alpha and omega – blood-scorched – I am wild tulip of Shiraz.

The highest terrace of Paradise is the sanctuary of: the Dervish.
The origins of Majesty lie in the honest service of: the Dervish.

The secret vault of talismans even jaded sight finds wondrous
is entered by that lightest door: the drooping eyelid of the Dervish.

The Glories before which the noon-crowned sun, in submissive
immolation, must set itself down – that is the horizon of the Dervish.

Those Palaces of cloud spectacularly overseen by angelic Rizvan
are no more than a crack in the plank of the door of the Dervish Eden.

Those beams redeeming dullest alloys, making gold of them instead,
are an alchemy one beholds only in the orbit of gently-tilted heads.

East to west, armies spring. But from Timeless birth to Timeless death
the Wind that swirls their fallen leaves is the circular Dervish breath.

That priceless Tapestry this world has yet to undo or thin – let this
be heard without elaboration: it is spun in the Dervish whirlwind.

When we daily plead at arch or altar taking forms of Persian Kings,
we only bend the knee because they serve beneath Dervish diadems.

Yes: whenever you loudly sing of conquest, you Emperor or Empress,
remember your golden neck is noosed in a Dervish ring of fortress.

If Karun's golden city, still, rusts underground – hear it told thus:
a revolutionary Dervish wrath delivered the tenfold downward thrust.

And when a King nears success in his very greatest venture,
to that whirling oval of a Dervish face it is but dimmest mirror.

Freely I am bound to the Asaf of our age: wisest vizier, whose glance
is Patronage. From the inward Dervish, his outward powers dance.

Reader: if you must find where darkest, deepest Endlessnesses well,
their utmost headwater is the lowest dust circling the Dervish cell.

Be circumspect. All that is material and immaterial evolves afresh
with respect to the centred foot, the revolving foot, of the Dervish.

43

Tonight – a perfume slides, sighs, down from the high rose garden.
I am one with Wine, the paradisial angel with eyes Joy-darkened.

Today – why shouldn't the vagabond bray of possessing kingdoms?
Field's wide fringe: his feasting place. Fleet cloud-shade: his pavilion.

In spring, the teaching grass blossoms each hill, and plain, with this:
the knowing Lover prefers, over future favours, to savour today's kiss.

With divine wine, enrich that palace of your heart. This world of tricks
has a mason for its grave-dust wall in which you'll be the six-foot brick.

Why kindle to unfaithful society? – you fail to gain a single glint
when your monastery candle is lit from the unbelievers' flagrant lint.

Hermit – don't write me off in your blotted log with wine in the vein!
Who knows with what watermarks Fate darkened books of brain?

Reader – though your homing bird be walked to death, still choose this
poet's line: for, down among wrong-most doings, I fly to Paradise.

This heart, in firing up for You, has scorched its chest entire –
as if a hearth had caught such flame the home became its torch.

That sun You are, by keeping distance, melts us bad enough. But
if we turn, in love, to that Perfection, our tinder with a puff goes up.

If any could glimpse one tip of braid looped against the Angel-face,
he and I would fulminate, as worlds of blood that collide in space.

How hard hearts burn! These tears are a bonfire to which I cupped,
last night, my heart's slim wick: licking Desire, that moth went up.

With much heat, it's hardly strange that warm-hearted Friends follow:
but, when I lose myself in such fevers, even a stranger's heart glows.

The Tavern-waters swept off my sackcloth clothes. In hot draughts,
that liquid red of the Tavern blazed constructed reason all to naught.

In the penitent kiln, my heart's clay cracked. With that, this flagon
of liver – for lack of Wine and Tavern – flared into a funeral urn.

So, don't scratch this itch with careful talk. See, to win Your lips,
in full view, how my sight disrobed – put a match to worldly gossip.

Reader – why steep yourself in prattle? Sip the wine that drowns.
Chattering teeth cause sleeplessness, and life's candle inches down.

45

Ensnared in Your thicket-hair, my heart flew there freely. So,
skewer that bird with a single Glance – it brought it upon itself.

I've learned that when Your bow-hand delivers yearning, there is no
escape from the kindly blow: through flight, that Arrow rights itself.

Sweet pyres of God, I swear by Your brightness: my fullest desire
through starless nights is that of the taper – to burn down with itself.

Nightingale: when, blossoming dark, you first noted Love, I declared:
When it comes to that self-willed, self-sung Rose – keep it to yourself.

This scent won't unmask itself like bartered musk along the Silk Road:
its bud holds, many-wrapped, robe-tight with fragrant-petalled Self.

Take your leave, then, of those who Lord it over straitened households –
the greatest ease in a home is, richly, to inhabit all corners of oneself.

Drink fire instead! I incinerate me, life the stake: yet I shall ever weld
to that lawful man and wife, the faithful family head, I am to myself.

You make pillow talk of this heart's matters of state. My Prince, again,
we retire to your rooms to assess the intimate moods of heart's provinces.

See how blatantly the spies of our adversaries lean in to glean some policy.
In reality, our secret's blown: no show of power here; only our love story.

This First – most sacred – night of the Word is rarer jewel than a comet's rise:
oh, to slumber together under angel skies, then wake to the dawn of your gaze.

Yes, I dived darkly for this blood-pearl, divinely soft in piercing: I yearned
to know it completely. In this oysterless world, who seeks such perfection?

Master, your night-whispers are zephyrs: a kind of morning to melt this ache.
Late, in moon-white gardens, I merge with perfume. My urgent bud breaks.

Hear, then, my highest wish: to praise and sweep, with blinking eyes, the dusty
Ways you keep; on dunes of desire, to turn each lash to a tiny broom of sighs.

Reader: fearing philistines, are you sure and able to stopper Love? Join me
at the generous table, forever pouring, until we drop, wilder wines of poetry.

Your tresses snare us either way: in hot distress or ardent prayer.
One lock suffices – a shaving, God-dark from His workshop floor.

True: such beauty as Yours thunders, miraculous with all Beauty –
but what is said about Your lightning eyes conjures only fantasy.

Those lips – they say – can empty tombs as surely as a Jesus kiss;
but then they claim Your ebony braid makes the unbreakable noose.

I name Your lips: *Holy River*. Only fools run to sip the ordinary
when – already within – waters spout sublime, plunge unstoppably.

When that cool eye opens, shout a hundred Amens: bless the look
that massacres numberless lovers without slightest flinch or blink.

In the study of Love, in its most wondrous precisions, I am precise.
I witness how even seven heavens can become hell, hell a paradise.

You think an evil tongue can wag its words, then exit without fear?
No. The Angelic log records – in duplicate – each sentence entire.

No sortie brings victory when any repel that sly siege of Your gaze:
Your glances jolt, as bolts from crossbows – forever lying in wait.

Reader: are you immune to that mane of curls and what it represents
when it has strewn the most careful heart, wrenched all observance?

Let the soul beat inward, outward, with quenching heat: that blood
of Grace. Veins of Grace. Liver of Grace. A living heart in flood.

Make of love a cup, a bowl, a flagon you may drink straight from:
you will intoxicate all with Love, and be called His drunken one.

Friends, vine's daughter repented: too long she'd veiled her face under leaf.
To that lame chaperone, Reason, she put her case: for us, her wine was freed.

Love, so long in store, was brought out – poured. We who laboured to relieve
our thirst, purified in sweat, ask the shameful: *Why would she keep us in need?*

Those dubious ones should take her in marriage, yield themselves up as dowry.
The intoxicant daughter hid for good reason – undoing by shielding her beauty.

But heart, be Love's minstrel enlivening again. Address our streets with sweet
refrains: ah, the drunken Winemaker presses fresh wine for the drunkard strain!

My clay nature; the Beloved breeze: together, these burgeoned a spring strung
with blossom. From fragrant petals, through a bulbul, rose our night-sung song.

Neither the flood of oceans, nor gaping infernos, could flush that wondrous hue
that the crushed grape stitches, as a bloody patch, in the Sufi's coarse-wool robe.

Part with pride, rank, wealth – offer your hand to humility's bride and groom.
The sand-filled coffers of faith, the blank heart, are what envy makes its own.

Would you possess the cosmos as a bauble, yet be its troubled grain?
Forget duplicitous sackcloth, the outward show: drink inward wine.

The Beloved is a beautiful nation that calls you to willing service.
If not, Her borders could not contain even Her smallest province.

In the Tavern, you cannot procure a drink if sobriety is your coin.
The prayer-mat tainted with piety turns the vintage in you to sand.

The censor scolds: *Keep far from Her wanton door! Avert your glance!*
Such cranial advice. The frass at Her heart's threshold speaks more sense.

So, rinse our variegated times from your coat. Would you think a wine great
that arrived in rainbowed hues? Drink in the single colour of that other world.

How simple the treasure-dive seemed: my boat by shallows; the weather fine.
I was in error: Her moonlit hills of swells roll in, drowning promised pearls.

But don't be lured by imperial pomp. It's dust. Yes, all grandeur solicits:
but what use is any crown if you must lose your lumpen head to win it?

Harbour yourself, then, against desire's fleet. Let no worldly face cast off
your heart. Those campaigns of pleasure begin with parades – end in grief.

Find instead the pricelessness waiting within, couched already in your oyster.
No heart should struggle through any straits – even for a continent of treasure.

Lookout to Self: astern, see how tight fists of cliffs knuckle down to horizon.
Your cargo is Her old, wise gold – and, of this, the miserly own not an atom.

Bleak blood we've bled through the eyes, down our cheeks
and yet nothing is seen. No flood alarm, no tidal warning.

Deep in our heart-chambers hatched smooth stones of love.
If their bold mother flies into storm, so must the fledglings.

We lowered faces into dust at the edge of the path the Friend
frequents, rewarded by dust if dust is what the Friend leaves.

Our weeping is a torrent that seizes even the stoniest heart,
tumbling it down these stairs of land, drunkenly out to sea.

How can I thirst, then, when I am this awash with myself?
I burst my dam to splash Your road, the hem of Your robe.

In envy, sunset shreds kindly clouds because my Moon has
swooned and roundly, whitely weaves for me a coat of light.

In the Wine-house street, this heart now pounds a purer beat:
it is a Sufi dancing here in my convent, gently, like a prayer.

51

In the shadow of night, a breeze journeys to whisper *you* to me.
I yield this heart, too, to go as that wind – whatever must be, Be.

I've endured to such a degree, I can confide in all that life provides.
At dusk, I sigh with lightning; dawn, I exclaim in wind's wide mouth.

Naked as a fresh-born brute my heart slept, curled in your den of hair.
It could never say into the shrouded ear: *Will you remember I'm here?*

But I understood today the substance in the teachings of Perfect Ones.
Love: may their inmost blood be overflooded by the good they've done.

Your memory arises in me – melts to slow-blood the heart within me –
when I see meadow-breeze tease loose the green turban of a rosebud.

Beloved: when wind in profuse coronation yellows narcissus in spring,
it is – to this heart – hollowly reminiscent of even your cap's regal rim.

Through finger and thumb, enfeebled, I lost my grip on life's slim cord
until, into my still cell, as a wild scent, sunrise slipped you: a single curl.

I trace my true birth to that night we were one. Youth passed, company
passes – here on earth, all that is not of you dims, or dies, with memory.

Rememberer: the mild heart bears in on its desire – leaves on a breeze.
Yes – the reward for right nature is to enter a leaf, depart as the breeze.

It is Your sun that makes each lovely reflection –
and Your face that animates beauty itself, loveliest One.

Caught up in the wind, that hair is God's falcon: the Grace-wing
of long pinion, a shadow sheltering the chicks of earthbound kings.

Those who choose not to reach for Your tresses – those thick tassels
of tresses – sooner than later shall, themselves, unravel and entangle.

And if the heart's blood cannot rise to Your cheek, it must forever
fester with the reek of liver.

                         Ah, Love: when Your eyes launch
their glance, this scarry heart is the willing shield in its arc –

and when Your ruby mouth, encrusted in sugar, kisses
our savoury dust, soul runs like honey – like this.

Instant upon instant, I am Your loving candle
that, hour by hour, Your kind sun rekindles.

My soul, with Your rays: aflame! May
all, in desire, be fuel for This blaze.

53

Last night, our words walked that long story of Your hair. Our circle became
a crown – each mouth a jewel recalling curls through night's most fecund time.

Returned from nothingness, every heart – those who'd bled from the tip of Your
eyelash – poured with desire to be pierced once more from Your eyebrow's quiver.

Love, forgive the wind its misdemeanours, for it bore Your message in. None other
came on Your behalf, and all would have fallen stiller than a leaf-fall in summer.

Quaker of worlds: world had no news of how You move, until Love's tender riot
tremored through. In that Mystery, all things cast a second shadow, invisibly true.

Love: with head in full sun, without a turban, my heart was on the safe path
once Your glossy tress had looped my ankle.

                                        So, loosen Your coat a little
and let this heart, encoiled there, thud openly with You as its hearth.

Love: lost in desire for Your face unveiled, I've passed from this
world. Will You let Your shadow kiss my tomb? Promise?

Noon's disunion, night's estrangement: these cease to apply to my Beloved.
This is the omen I cast beneath a passing comet.

Dense with grace and beauty, this seasonal world fooled me; but the lingering
peace of a true Master became my fall, my spring.

Now, in the world, heart gives its light unresisting to horizons. Hearts can rise
as suns do, when dust that caused all grief adores.

To hope that arrives at first knell of day, that knelt behind screens of mist, say:
Come out – the doings of night could never persist.

Praise the Creator for this, who spills dawn's petals from rosy crowns to quell
the fuss of December's gusts and the august thorn.

Stumbling forlorn through the pitch thickets of midnight Hair – gone. In bone
and blood, the rumbles of interminable storm: gone.

I was prey the holy Locks ensnared; but a familiar cheek of hill arose as Guide
from that forest to loosen each grievous knot inside.

Now, in union with my Love, I march to the Wine-house with harp and drum
and the story I sing has nothing to do with separation.

Cup-bearer: you poured with such wrenching tenderness, my wine-sickness
is stanched. May the vine ever kiss your goblet's brim!

Reader: there is no bill for this, no itemisation of Truth. I feel only relief
beyond limit, as one who passes through Love, or Death.

55

In that just-before, half-lit dawn, the Perfect Masters bought my freedom.
Dust-whipped, They brought Eternal Water under a parched quarter-moon.

Then fuller Sun broke through in essence, to which They made me senseless
mist. They bore from horizon a chalice from which I could drink blessedness.

Under the auspices of morning, in that relief of Light, because of that Night
of Power, a commanding Vine was fused to my stock by God's own knife.

Then an angel, bloodlessly white, brought news: that whatever tyrannies
would malign me, the patience of the Perfect Masters would flood me.

At last, They had aligned my mirror of self and the beauteous Mirror
to face one another, so my soul could tread God's endless corridors.

I passed from myself, tremulous, the Beloved soul welling my face.
They told of God's destructive Daughters, the futile idols of blood.

So, I gain my desire, my heart a full red moon. Why wonder at it?
My cause was worthy: They gave me all, in charity without limit.

All this honey drenching, the sweetness overtaking my words, stems
from what They put in my patient earth: my lovely branch of sugarcane.

It's impossible to lose, I say, once They bestow endurance: the enemy may
seem to win, may even show clemency, yet to perseverance must surrender.

Lead becomes precious in service to an Elder Master: I began as lowly dust;
now I am lifted with the mountain winds…

They led me to undying life that day: breath by breath, all kinds of death
died within me – They unwrote me, so I could quote the deathless You.

They shooed my soul towards Your locks, as if Your hair were a tree
at dusk and I were Your wayward flock circling air. They saved me.

Now I scatter myself like sugar for the world, because They gave
me that true Beloved whose fluid limbs are boned by sweetness.

Yes – how the early-risers breathed each prayer, how blessed
I was, when They unbound me, finally, from Time's duress.

Night of Power: 'On this night, [Muslims] believe that prayers are
specially answered.' (Clarke, p.236)

'A lovely woman, Shakh-i-nabat (branch of sugarcane), who snatched
the heart of Hafiz in the vigour of his youth.' (Clarke, p.41)

Before daybreak secured its world, gossamer angels were at the Tavern door.
They brought out Adam's breath, kneaded to shapes in which love could froth.

They – who flit beyond heavenly screens, respecting limits imposed on spirit –
showered wine-drops upon me: this dust that fasted, unattached, beneath a tree.

Sky's brittle chalice could not contain such intensities of Love: so they cast lots
to see how best my helplessness might be firmed into forms that do a little work.

Peace surged up thickly between me and God, for which these sloe-eyed angels
forged my grateful cup.

My mind was once a dusk field whose sheaves seemed
looming centurions: of this, one ear, in whispering, vanquished vigilant Adam.

But our seventy-two factions excuse us all: when Truth eludes their flapping,
they jostle instead for feebler perches.

Our earthly bonfires the candle scoffs;
for true Flame, the moth harvests itself in a searching, flesh-fluttering flash.

God, with holy blood, moulds the heart of the corner-sitter cowering from
tyrannies into the mole, lovely on the beloved cheek, all eyes alight upon.

Reader: since that time the brides of Speech first combed their knotty,
tipsy hair, who has better bared the Mind behind its veils of thought?

'In all, there are seventy-two sects of Islam…' (Clarke, p.408)

57

After the contraction – benumbed – a cataract of wine
within! In spate – again – the current sparkles inside.

I raise a thousand praises to that rush of crimson that
flushed every atom of jaundice from my complexion.

The art of plucking the fruit as if vines were an emerald
harp; the nimble heels, crushing… may these never spoil.

Fate pruned me for Love: whatever Fate plants in our soil,
no one can grub out.

                    Don't use your last breath for wisdom:
whether outcast or philosopher, death will have you stumped.

So, censor, take your braying elsewhere. Ours is not the farm
God intended you to work.

                    Rather, breathe such calm that when,
at last, eyes grow dark, mourners claim: *This cannot be the end.*

Be content. At least, practise contentment. Of loss, win, make
no display. Take pains, and Time will be satin on your back.

Reader: the First Day made us each a soundless vessel.
Drain it. Drunk with Unity, drink to purify yourself.

Last night, in retreat, God turned me outside in: my worship, dry
and outwardly, was put away; my inward weave, steeped in Wine.

Earlier, in reverie, my mistress in youth appeared to me – churned,
in the ashen cauldron of the old man, the younger man's concerns.

This young Master – a glory approaching Glory – an honest brigand
of heart – began to stalk, instead, God… soon walked dead to all else.

The glow of that Rose's complexion out-glossed my songbird's quills.
My moth, nearing the Candle's chuckle, flared to a brief face of flame.

At dawn, there was weeping. At dusk, weeping. But not a tear that fell,
out of sleepless cloud, was ever forgotten. Each perfect drop was a pearl.

So, the rash Sufi who, yesterday, dashed cup on pitcher till little was left
had – by nightfall, with a single draught of wine – returned himself to Self.

The Cup-bearer it was – that pristine flower – whose power entranced us:
we read scripture in our circle as if we were petals in an opening narcissus.

Reader: see how a humble cell becomes a banqueting hall for the One when
to the Loveheart's pulse heart skips and, to the Lovebird's tune, soul hums.

Last night, my Beloved rose to me: a full white moon.
That cheek's cold light singed my heart.

The One for whom overwhelming Lovers and overturning
cities seem as natural as pulling off a robe.

The One to whom each soul is a reason for being Sun – these
shreds of smoke and cloud to be reabsorbed.

Those black distractions of hair lour over stony faith – to draw
greater attention to that incandescence of Face.

Ah, these eyes have expended what blood in me heart mustered.
Love should account such tears as profit, as loss.

What can be given, then, to one whose soul is removed? Silver
is deemed dull, set against the plenty-coloured coat.

The One spoke outwardly – *I'll despatch you at my whim*. Yet
an inward glance flashed unseen to this fire within.

Then whispers, serenely whispered: *Love, let burn this mortal
cloak*. Beloved, oh: who taught You such love?

'To be clothed in one colour is the Persian idiom for sincerity.' (Bell, p.164)

If this heart, in desire, cranes forever for
Forever-lips – what, then, is Desire?

This cup of yearning, its filling Love,
I offer up – cupped inside the soul.

One who fights against holy curls
tightens the apprehending loop.

To the rosy cheek, Beloved entices:
but sleek blue-blackness interposes.

Couched so close, embroiled in
that mane, who thinks of standing?

Perhaps now, side by side, finally,
You can tell me Your name…?

Pleasure is this moment's meeting
ensnared among eternities of sheets.

Company constellates the happy ones:
but this secret heart carries a secret Sun.

Rightful One – how shyly sky sips dawn's flood from Your cup!
Your enemy's heart is a tulip, dark-streaked, steeped in blood.

No human, however high-minded, can scale Your peak: even
imagination's fleetest mountaineer might climb a million aeons.

Your mass of curls is lamp and sight to this world. On zephyrs
of fortune, one ringlet slips over each soul, as if a wedding band.

You are the moon, full and bright in that starry dome of justice.
Both eye and light to a whole world. Perfect goblet; purest wine.

When Venus herself inclines, in piercing light, to sing Your praises,
those who envy You are instant companions in loss and weeping.

The nine rings of day and night, their medallions in gold and silver,
are nothing but the humblest items in Your open vault of treasures.

Into verse – mind's virgin daughter – You breathed, whispered wide
secrets; let the dowry of worlds, of this matchless bride, be Yours.

Here, Your humblest writer metes out devotion in metres. An infinite
kindness witnesses the pact. Servant-loving, You sign with an ocean.

On her straight branch of cypress, again, the bulbul kisses
with what she cries: *Let no eye's evil brush the rosy cheek!*

Beloved rose, don't be aloof with such singers. You unfurl
to innermost desire: in thanks, then, receive a fevered lover.

All through the songless silence, I gave out no grievance:
so long as absence is absent, presence cannot be present.

The outwardly yearn for angels, cloudy palaces – we hold
the Wine-house as palace, the Beloved its angels of Paradise.

Drink to the lilt of the harp, offer up no grief. If any condemn
such glugging as sinful, reply: *Ah, but it is God who pardons.*

Others may take pleasure in pleasures or be glad of gladness;
for us, joy's one source is that grieving love for the Beloved.

Faithful Sun, why complain when apart from your Moon?
Aloneness breeds oneness. Nightfall seethes with light.

Shapely Cypress – with such grace You lean with the wind.
At any instant, centurions of need shall kneel here for favours.

Your form alone is an auspice, weaving eternities. Without bend:
Your silhouette. Destiny tailors elegant shadows to Your contour.

To those who desire the hyacinth fragrance of Your tresses, I say:
Consume yourself in fire. As aloeswood, smoulder exquisitely.

Those who watch, to scold me, cannot adjust my value. I am
proof: pliant in the jaws of their shears, yet gold nonetheless.

The moth flutters away his heart in the heart of the candle:
without Your countenance, my old core gutters nothingness.

Any heart that flies to You for sacred news finds a Holy Place,
Your safe enclosure: no longer desires to walk counterclockwise.

Instant to instant, what gain can there be in offering from my eyes
cleansing rains, if I cannot couch, like a prayer, within Your arch?

The Sufi who, last night, lacking You, darkly shunned all wine,
at dawn grew tipsy, seeing Your tavern door so brightly in reach.

Like that vessel, lifted, dizzy with vapours at the rim of the pitcher,
I rattled all evening, sipping rich mysteries from Your dripping lip.

My heart swoons, as though You were a woman who comes voluptuously
singing: a muddler of colours, inconstant, whirling veils swirling doom – murderous.

Those who turn their face to the Moon, waxing to holy fullness as they
look, prefer thoughtless rags to the garments of observance, the long robe of austerity.

Grateful, in beauty's sport, that You dominate the angels in all forms
of possession, You take the winner's cup, splash Adam's ashes with clearest liquor.

I came to Your palace as one derelict, ruined. One leaf was enough
from pity's tree. Attached to nothing, I find myself attached deeply to Love.

Now, under that Word whose utterance kindles devotion's pyre,
I'm no longer the slave to speech and thought that dwindles those fires.

As I wept last night, an invisible emissary visited me, saying:
Why rage against destiny? Accept each bright stage of difficulty.

We keep such pride in our own powers! It is written: *Only*
through the Sower are kings grown and matters burgeoned.

Place, then, the salving cup in my grave: on that last dawn
of awakening, this Wine will quell my springs of terror.

Reader, remember: no cloud lies between you and Love.
Rise! Unwind your shroud. You are yourself the veil.

Bulbul flies in, long in the tongue – sings all day that Rose should requite.
Rose stays tight: a budded thought of how she might sway most gracefully.

Ah – not every Beauty erodes its beholder beautifully.
A boulder enfurled in moss can be Master of its place.

Here, in ruby hearts, blood bursts at the battering waves of world:
the shaved and shivered stone, in loss, shatters its embedded gem.

Rose is wedded, stem and bloom, to bulbul's tuneful kiss.
Weren't it so, no beak could break in such bleak tenderness.

The Beloved traverses wastes: heart's caravans flock in that direction. Though
travel imperils, the deeper one ventures, the more protection hastens to follow.

Reader – if you creep down the Beloved's street, beware:
skull's white stone will meet there walls harder than itself.

Heart, whether or not you stir through night over money or health,
give pause to consider how Love is cut, and cuts, to catch the Light.

Shrug lust away – I mean, what ugliness adheres to lust:
trust, instead, the gardened bed held in sight of the Rose.

If, with one weak sip at the cup, Sufi can't help but tweak his cap a little dozily,
see how wine in draughts blows his turban, laughing as it flies, flapping slowly.

Beloved, Your holy shape, so natural to these eyes, is mine
in unrelenting dowry. Heart: why seek, as mistress, misery?

From Love's tavern, under full moon, an emissary of vapour came:
a zephyr, with little to say – *Drink up! The prohibition is lifted.*

Divine judgement, ever busy with itself, is drifting down: see
its pristine angel, mercury-tongued in silent word of amnesty.

Misdoing is eclipsed by God's forgiveness: that's a pliant
matter no mind can bend to. Brain, why chatter? Quiet!

Carry reason to the tavern, flat in its perforated flagons.
Let its clotting blood be brought to sparkling fountains.

The Rare Ones never clutch at heaven: nevertheless,
heart, if in darkness, make every effort at endeavour.

Together: my cheek and the grime of the tavern floor.
As one: this key of hearing, those lovely locks of Hair.

That One whose faith blinds the cruel father, who flings
as a wind the bolted tavern door, looses angel tongues…

… He is quenched to the ninth heaven, quickened, burnt
in the ways of God. May the evil gaze bypass His bones.

This extravagance in Love has no meanness in it, no trite
trace – seen from above, its lowest stoop is faultless flight.

Whatever aroma this soul has, spills from that cheek.
My inner bloodline I will trace, track back to that blush.

The high excellence in dark-eyed angels they think unique
is more meekly explained as what must arise in that soft cheek.

The cypress is a fallen statue, mud-wracked, neck broken, astonished
at my Beloved's form. Rosebud, seeing a Petal so lush, departs its bush.

With filigree body, in embarrassment, jasmine twists at those supple limbs,
that unsullied white. Swarming shame, Judas tree squats in jealous blood.

Just as rosewater gathers its ghosts of fragrance by begging a blessing
from God, so does the musk-pod guess its perfume from that tress.

Sunrays choke in coveting smoke at the intensity of Your gaze.
Moon shrinks to a sickle sliver at Your cheek's purer silver.

The poet, at peak strength, may trickle a sap that leaks into hearts;
but souls are dews that fuse and run, one Drop, the length of that cheek.

Each dawn, for that perfect scent of rose, I flew to the garden.
Heart burst, like the bulbul's, I sought some remedy for brain.

I gazed at the flushed bloom. Those flickering petals of flame,
in my benighted skull, glowed brighter than any worldly ember.

So glad in freshness and beauty was that blossom, that the heart
of the bird in me, hive of a million refrains, went restlessly silent.

Enviously, narcissus dropped its head, brewed up a sweat, brow
spangling dew; tulip grew hotly veined, stained in heart and soul.

The voluble lily took offence, unsheathed its long tongue of threat;
anemone, like a man with two women, cleared a duplicitous throat.

See me now, stooped at the cask, goblet heart brimming worship.
Ah, watch me grow clear, wine-bearer to inebriates, a glassy cup.

Youth and pleasure are the plucking of a rose – no more, no less.
I can say this. In the purest messenger, there is only the message.

Holy traveller – we have cut a new path to the highest garden. There, fresh wines
pour to our heart; together, we disperse time's petals, inwardly, split sky's dome.

Armies may shed loving blood, raise towers of grief; yet the cup-bearer and I
shall relieve the earth of such hordes, peeling them up and away by a corner.

Wine isn't given, always, full bitter-strength: at times, a draught is thinned
with rosewater. Wind's censer spins few heads with intense rose incense.

In your hand, I'm a sweet-strung instrument. Make ever-sweeter songs
in me. We dance – palms up, head down – one loving, involuntary body.

Breeze, loft me, as You do all dust, to that high cloudlet of the Beloved. My
speck, unnoticed, might glimpse the Kingdom of lovely ones, dripping wisdom.

One preens vain intellect; another is the very loom for stuffy gossip. Let both try
themselves before the Just Ruler.

If you're looking for Eden, aspire – to the Tavern.
Drain its wine-jar: plunge into the Lake of Good; forget yourself at heaven's spring.

Beloved, Your true face is the glow in those far-off faces here convened: a row of
sated roses I sing for, with Love the tune and Love the tapping foot I put breath to.

Who, among us now, can tell the God-first sense in verse or, across a glib globe,
that weighted, well-placed Word? Reader: join me, in that necessary, other world.

In a hidden chamber of my heart resides a sweet One. A silk cheek, a hook
of curl – and I begin to spark and shudder inside like the hammered horseshoe.

Across the street, they look and shout: *Waster! Profligate! Wine-lover!* All true.
We drinking companions, unworldly spirits, keep mild eyes wide, dark with You.

Hold me here, languid in the liquid fall of Your locks, and, with easy sighs, I'll
stop dawn rising – no sun will come to comb the unkempt dark from Your hair.

Dare even the tiniest step towards the drunkards' den and You'll find me there,
ready, with wines unwatered, the stanzas honeyed.

When the Master arrives like this, that fine old face bearing a splendid beard
of reddish gold, my jaundiced face, likewise, turns aurous.

Those bows of Your tresses deliver glances in volleys: in my heart, already
wounded, so many targets remain, desiring the delicious calamity.

One tip of plait I grip with both hands; another is held by the Master:
for years, to and fro, this way and that, I thought that rope a tug of war.

Bliss and hopelessness slip equally, finally, away – as sand of two kinds.
Is it not best, then, to hold to one's heart, as though happy with its world?

As one parched by long night who first sights the new moon
and, tipping its heavenly cup, breaks his fast of light – I am.

For two or three dusks, I made myself a cup without wine. Such
an error should cause the vessel – even of beaten metal – to blush.

Never again, sober seclusion – even to serve as a pupil's example.
Sombre duty is that chain zealots place around the dervish ankle.

The city's chief of conscience, in saintly posture, gushes advice
by the quart. I sipped there once – now my shut lips thwart him.

I adore those – where do they go? – who spill red life on the wine
-house floor. I'd pour this mind towards their feet till pride expires.

Today I drink – though my wide shoulders carry prayer-mat's piety.
I worry if anyone will notice how there are always these two of me.

Everyone says: *Return to cold conscience – drink his wordy fires!*
But I've drained God's quieter glass, older than a thousand elders.

Ah, pupil of my eye, on your journey, hear this: *When your love*
exceeds its rim, tilt that cup gently, so all may live and drink with you.

If the very sun were my son, still I'd thank him to seek advice. With life
all but cold in them, the old grow bright with words. Listen. Grow old too.

Love won't pause to dangle any chain of Light around philosophy's wrist or
the reasonable neck. Abandon abstinence – then fondle the Beloved tress.

In prayer, worried beads and mottled cloak, in themselves, put no 'yes'
in bone or blood. Be importunate, instead, at the Wineseller's door.

For those who befriend God comes a transcending of the material.
Expend a hundred lives to find the True love: this is no idle counsel.

Evil's epitome amasses along the path. Our waysides throng with lies.
Keep eyes ahead. Press heart's message-hungry ear to the angelic conch.

All means meet with ruin. Young today; tomorrow, a sigh. Spine clenches
to a curve, a harp bewailing Time. Yet, how youthfully heart's drum thumps!

So: let the Wine-bearer's full purity be drunk.
I'm blessed by dregs. May bubbling cups ever lean towards me, with a wink.

When that One passes by, long tunic scattering gold in inebriant flakes, each
in genuine poverty feels the fatherly kiss – like a snow-sliver on the cheek.

Spring. Its first rose animates all, shatters penitence as a stone thrown
into the pool. Those soft petals pull the black taproot from this heart.

Morning stirs. The rosebud breaks out of itself: splits its green shirt
and, bulging with love, opens.

       Heart: learn from the rose's dewy diadem. Be clear
as that water. Grow as the cypress by pasture, in upright freedom.

The Bride is exactly this rosebud. Those eyes are jewels of dew.
In that wide smile, I dissolve myself – as faith into heart must do.

Who doesn't grieve for their rose? That screech of fraught bulbul,
the shrill from birds of a thousand elegies, echoes in every eyeball.

True – spring winds may bring a burnt smell; but agitations enliven
the petal. See how breezes jostle hyacinth hair on the nape of jasmine.

So, Reader, follow the melody of the holy minstrel, the harmony of the elder.
Time has only one song, one story: it disappears, a drop of water, in purest Wine.

74

Everywhere I go, they point and say: *There's the one who plays at Love.*
These eyes don't taint with ill-seeing: they always get worse than they give.

Being me, I meet contempt with faithfulness, tolerance, a tranquil temperament.
Observance of the law… means what? Muttering behind doors is faithlessness.

I went to the Master of the Wine-house, asking: *How may I save myself?*
He called for the flagon, and said: *Cover this – keep Love mysterious.*

From living in this illusory Eden, what might we learn? He replied:
Via that pupil, so dark at the centre of its prinked flower, pluck Light.

To dash the image I'd hung in the murk of myself, I poured new wine on
internal waters. Those pictures, gashed. I began to look not at – but through.

The tips of Your hair flare into tiny snake-like tongues: yet I truss, there, my life.
What value, otherwise? To strive without the Beloved is just another form of dust.

To brush the cheek of the proper friend is a hand halfway to that loveliest of faces.
To be familiar with every holy feature is a peek at the map for the Beloved place.

We can change the rein on ourselves, find a way to the Tavern's occupation.
Those who bray hardest against us tend to be the ones who feign vocation.

Speaker: to sip the Word of love, press lips to that unmarred Mouth; for
toasting those who boast austerity will only tar your tongue to its roof.

You – oh You who trail through the world such bridal trains of hair…
You're here! You followed a cord of pity that brought You to my door.

Quick: rein in Your disdain. Let's break with custom so I may prosper.
Haven't You come, after all, to me – the one who is a sultan of needs?

I'm a cone, fallen to the foot of Your sturdy cypress. Whether You've
arrived to kill me, a stag in Your forest, or to save me – You've come.

Before existence, beyond non-existence, You were the ruby Mouth. Too
strange, Your mixing of elements: if those Lips part, lava and ocean pour.

Amen upon Your quiet heart. Soundless as a fawn You move through
prayer, silent in that thicket, towards the hunter You felled with a glance.

My austerity: weightless as air upon air. Heavy, You come for plunder
to this, my most private place – to my heart, staggering and restless.

Your glimpse is as lightning to my innermost thunder. I'm jealous –
that these very same storm-heads benefit strangers. Still, rain is rain.

I come to myself… my lips are saying: *See how this state you're in
drips with wine. Do you return from the sacrifice drunk or zealous?*

The rose breaks fast, and opens. Unresisting, I bear it into me – dark wine.
In this season, where is a rose-cup without petals, a petal lacking sheen?

If your soil is a dust of self-denial, the rosebud heart surely shrivels.
Gardener, irrigate your plot with wine – let every bud swell a little!

See, today, the Sufi – who, yesterday, spoke so solidly on the need
for moderation – out wobbling in the fields, enamoured of the wind.

These smooth-cheeked blooms won't last the week: to come and go is
their nature. Nectar-drinker, you must hurry, as a bee does, to your rose.

Fellow lover: spring is in departure, and your rosebush yellows, untended.
The Beloved wine, like your garden's insect music, drains away, unheeded.

Our flock, darkly asleep among the trees, awaited dawn: it came like a cup, up
-side-down, reflecting a Face filling with light, Light dripping at a nick in its lip.

See: the Master is also the Minstrel, plucking sky's instrument to impossible rain.
That truer Sun for field and garden sings Love's banquet, again, onto empty tables.

In my mind, I re-make You: One of moonish form, with perfect arch of brow.
I will picture, somewhere, that down so fresh on Your cheek – as if on a petal.

I hope that what I order You to be, within me, privately, will fly as an arrow to
fall as rain: sky's fertile ink, everywhere signing Your name, bearing Your title.

I lift head from hands, allow sight to burn for You like noonday sand – every
part of me, all thought and perception, in thrilled assembly, squirms in heat.

But You put a sword to it, in that final place only the lovely ones understand:
the head that cast You in its image lies rocking at Your foot.

In its severed moment, a wearied, worried heart meets Truth.
In that fiery instant, I set light to my many-coloured coat – find infinite relief.

Now, wherever I sleep, the Beloved face hangs there. In my secret chambers:
a full, white moon. What need have I for distraction, then, that illusory star?

This heart was a dervish steed: it shook its mane, unruly, until taken by Love.
My holy Rider had no greed for crown or throne: only desire to win me over.

The most difficult lesson arrives: separation and union, too, are one – moon
to sun. If the Friend approves union, live in union; if separation, separation.

On that telling day I pass into death, make my coffin cypress:
then, even this material self will be flung to highest embrace.

Reader: let your rowboat press out from its harbour – a speck aswim in the Now.
The fishes will rise, bobbing like corks, bubbling pearls from ever-open mouths.

In the same way that morning stirs the air, I must tell my story
of longing. Evening brings my reply: *Rely on the glorious Wind.*

No pen can divulge the immensities, the mysteries of Love: such
ardour, even in its coolest voice, lies past the far edge of narrative.

Ensnare your heart in the beloved Hair. Become loon to that lovely,
open Look. Declare your Love, for careful words only hurt the lover.

Oh, Joseph – so preoccupied with Egypt! Ask Jacob, ask the Father,
how far filial love can go.

That temptress glance relieves – or agonises.
Encoiled among the prodigious tresses, one can meet famine with ease.

The material world is aflush with beauty and age, but carries no drop
of concern. Why go to it, enraged with flesh, to learn the next step?

The world's a marketplace. To find any profit in it, any grace, wish
for the consummate contentedness, that upward state, of the dervish.

Dervish: your purpose is a treasure to which the key is prayer. In you,
dawn's promise meets its dusky sigh, and the heart's Possessor appears.

Beloved Bird, flying alone, how long must You pick at unworthy bones?
Why does Your shadow, Fate, gild the worldly?

                              Reader – I keep my heart
from the beauties of this plane: they turn us back to this world, from That.

May these verses rise to a whirling dervish, up, till every soul links hands.
Dance – you blackened eyes of Kashmir, you flashing eyes of Samarkand!

Through late nights in which I remember, for as long as this long Night stands,
while lutes of two or three strings, with the singer, resound among themselves…

Let blessings fall: as warm drops fat with love, on the valley the Lover lives in,
on that calm tree the Beloved is, to my humble hut perched on a hump of sand.

For every walker who must roam this world, I send holy words, up, towards
the heavens. On their behalf, I'm firm in prayer.

                                        God, with every sword
one must confront, in every place one turns the cheek – protect us there.

No heart should wail in grief. We turn in the coils of Beloved hair:
each planet perturbed in its motion one day settles in that sphere.

No one hears the heavy footfall of Death. Let me die of Love:
if foresight could be mine, I'd know when dying turns to Life.

Your utterness, moment upon moment, reprieves. However
hard the conditions, remembering You softens the instance.

Till the Last Day, let this heart be as the sun's liver: densely
black with consuming Love!

                        How did I gain such noble descent,
but through You? A weave of wrong smells, of waste, was my life.

From that luminous down gracing Your face, every beauty is woven.
In marshalling our fragmented time, may You become the centurion.

Bless that potent Painter, who can gaze upon an unbearable Moon
to score, for the blinded, its thin crescent of mystery and promise.

The Beloved is vital: only those Fingers keep, from instant loss,
the material.

What is there to ask? The Beloved counts every
dot of Love: all that dust within, without. For me, that's enough.

I leaned in for a kiss – drained Beloved lips with sipping.
From source to delta, I plant one foot in life's deep river.

Nothing, no one, comes near to what I am tasting. I live
to convey the mystery, but must carry that wine in a sieve.

This cup in my chest fills again at the holy Mouth: happy wound!
The dawn rose flushes blood, sweats dew, to glimpse a higher bloom.

That flawless rose tore itself, root and thorn, from far hills to this throne
in the garden: the stern mats we fold away, by its green light, turn into buds.

A glance into the flooded wine-cup will see the world both whole and passing.
Lost in such drinking, who will remember Jamshid, or any other worldly King?

So, minstrel moon: raise in me a tide of music – lengthen those fingers of light
to play this harp of bones; caress my veins as though they were bright strings.

For those too full with the wine of earth, with themselves, there is merely
the staggering – bring them wine of a different kind, and eyes soon clear.

When vein and bone, all flesh and brain, are awash with what unbloodily
bleeds from Love, it's only soul confirming its intimate terms with body.

The mindful owl seems to stall incoming light with its brash *Who-You?*
Seize dawn's goblet with both hands: hear one cry *I Am!*, another *Alas!*

Heart – be a lunatic sun, leaping in pursuit of your whitely setting Love.
Run to the level horizon: there, look in the eyes of every deathless Lover.

Share elixir with the bending gardener. With that fine Sultan who tends
the rose, grow slow with wine. Toast authority first – freedom, later on.

Now I swallow words that rise too quick. Reader – learn from the reed,
tongued by that blessed aether, writing its tonguelessness into the breeze.

CODA

Beloved, where among the rocks is announcement of our union, so I may fly?
I am Eden's bird, ensnared by this world: let me ascend through earthly gravity.

Call me, Your slave, and I vow by all Desire to leave behind – below as above –
this love of power: let ours be the means by which the slave gains highest dignity.

Master, each drop from Your cloud is a counselling word, a cooling mercy. Pour
on me now, before I'm unwound like a grit turban, borne up, thinning to vapour.

Holy traveller: when you visit my stone, bring along both wine and songster –
I'll dance that shroud to twists and twirls, stoked into smoke by divine incense.

I am old. Nonetheless, my Love, take me to You: one night, in intimate grasp.
In the first cold gasp of dawn, I'll arise from You, made young in Your embrace.

You are true Self: neither sky's threats nor brutal time can render two from One.
All wealth is dust at the base of Your ladder – at Your breath, I'll scale the rungs.

Love, how can my humble sapling inch itself into elegant Cypress, that high crown?
Lift me from worldliness. Pinch me out, and away, between Your finger and thumb.

'This ode is inscribed upon the tomb of Hafiz.' (Bell, p.176)